Successful Leadership through the Government of 12

Revised Edition

Cesar Castellanos

CESAR CASTELLANOS D © 2003
Published by G12 Editors
sales@g12bookstore.com

ISBN 1-932285-03-2

All Scripture quotations are from the NEW KING JAMES VERSION of the Bible. Copyright 1979, 1980, 1982 by Thomas Nelson Inc., publishers. Used by permission.

Revised edition, *Successful Leadership through the Government of Twelve,* originally published as *Leadership of Success Through the Group of Twelve,* in 1999 by:

1st Edition	Editorial Vilit &Cia. Ltda. 1999
	Calle 22 C No. 31-01
	Santa Fe de Bogotá, D.C.
	Colombia – South America
Reprinted	Jubilee Christian Center
	175 Nortech Parkway
	San Jose, CA 95134 USA
2nd Edition Revised	G12 Editors. 2003
	2020 NE 163rd St.
	Suite 101 Miami Fl. 33162
	USA

Printed in Colombia

DEDICATION

This book is dedicated to the One who chose me even before my birth and was pleased to reveal His son to me; to the One who cancelled the death decree that the adversary raised against me; and, further, to the One who did not allow the vision to end at its inception. To the One who Daniel referred to as, "The ancient of Days," I dedicate this book to.

You are the most important Being in my life and I love you with all of my strength.

To my beloved wife Claudia, who has been one of the greatest blessings from God to me, since we have battled together in the ministry, and she has always characterized herself as a sensitive woman guided by the Holy Spirit.

I love you with the love that only the Lord can give.

CREDITS

So many people have had a hand in the making of this book that naming them individually would be practically impossible. However, I would like to express my appreciation to the following: Youth Ministry of the International Charismatic Mission, in particular, Pastors Cesar and Claudia Fajardo for their invaluable contribution to the vision; each member of the pastoral team who, as personal friends have watched over the purity of the doctrine; my wife Claudia for her advice and contributions which have been of great value; my four daughters, who were always a great support and encouragement; the editorial team; and each member of the church without whom this book would lack refinement.

Finally, because of the unwavering dedication to the Lord that each contributor possessed, it was therefore possible for the vision to gain force.

Cesar Castellanos D.

CONTENTS

PART III
CELLULAR VISION:
21ST CENTURY REVOLUTION

FOREWORD

As I travel the world, it becomes increasingly evident that we are living in the last days and that God is pouring out His Spirit upon the earth in an unprecedented manner. The world is beginning to take notice as the church takes a rightful place in that great end time army, establishing His Lordship in places of government, local communities, work places and most of all the home.

Dr. Cesar Castellanos is one of those young men God has raised up who is on the cutting edged of an awesome move of God in Bogotá Columbia.

I would like to recommend his book *"Successful Leadership Through the Government of Twelve."*

In part one, Dr. Castellanos incorporates the two major aspects of vision and leadership, describing how they are independent but complimentary one to the other. He further describes with practical wisdom and insights the fundamental importance and qualities of a successful leader.

In part two he shares various personal life experiences relative to the social and spiritual needs of his own country of Columbia, South America, emphasizing the positive impact that they have made, believing that any country can be transformed when using the principles established in this vision together with the word of God and guidance of the Holy Spirit.

In part three, Dr. Castellanos continues to detail his vision for the ministry of cellular groups, noting with great clarity how each Believer is called to live and operate in the Kingdom of God based on Matthew 10:1, *"And when he had called unto his twelve disciples, he gave them power over unclean spirits, to cast them out, and to heal all manner of sickness and all manner of disease."*

I believe that the vision he has outlined in this book can revolutionize and empower the church all over the world to take cities and nations to God.

The growth of our church and the growth of Christianity throughout the nation of South Korea did not come by accident. It came through fervent, violent and prevailing prayer, of which the foundation of the foundation of the vision is made. As Jesus said in Matthew 11:12, *"The kingdom of heaven suffers violence and the violent take it by force."* Until recently, it took great sacrifice to be a Christian in South Korea. But now at least one-fourth of our nation, are believers in the Lord Jesus Christ. The church in Colombia is experiencing a similar impact. Our Lord is truly moving all over the world.

As you read through the pages of this timely message and embrace this cell vision, you too will be challenged and encouraged to move into a non-traditional concept of church and ministry. *"Unless the Lord builds the house, they labor in vain who built it"* (Psalm 127:1).

Dr. David Yonggi Cho
Yoido Full Gospel Church
Seoul, South Korea

INTRODUCTION
LEADERSHIP WITH A PURPOSE

I am thoroughly convinced that the days in which we live are days of change and that God in a sovereign manner is awakening in us a leadership centered around Himself and the establishing of His kingdom on the earth. Unfortunately, the primary objective of many leaders is to forge ahead with leadership that is centered on them. When do we need leadership with a Christ-centered purpose? When members of the community are apathetic towards the development of the same, when the leader feels he has lost his authority, or when the leadership of a community is in the hands of people lacking godly character.

The world is looking for leaders with integrity, serving as examples in not only the religious community, but in every arena of life. I am certain that when a man can lead his family into the right path and fully places his trust in God, success will be imminent.

How many leaders have initiated the development of a specific dream or vision from the Lord with great zeal and enthusiasm; and have seen it to completion? I would dare say many have started, but not many of them have successfully completed it. I have been to so many different places in the world and the thing that has surprised me most is the large numbers of people passing through churches who have not ultimately persevered to make an impact in their communities. This is a result of a leadership crisis.

There are great sophisms designed to distract and divert leaders from the objectives pre-established by God for their lives. As a result of this, I believe the time has come to give purpose to the vision that is in the heart of God, being watchful of the danger of falling into conformity through achieving relative success.

Our Lord Jesus Christ, before departing this world, said to His disciples, *"All authority has been given to Me in heaven and on earth. Go therefore and make disciples of all nations."* With that directive, the Lord was revealing His divine will of salvation and discipleship for all men. It is not enough for a person to hear the gospel or to attend a church.

We must turn each one of them into a true disciple of Jesus Christ. Many preachers take the message of the gospel to remote places and multitudes come forward to profess their faith in Christ. But for lack of effective follow-up in their respective communities, the harvest is eventually lost.

If there isn't follow-up for those who make a decision for Christ, we are concentrating all our efforts on something that will not last. We have to work with a defined purpose, understanding that leaders, who compromise with God, live for the present time. Nevertheless, God is entrusting us not only for the evangelization of the world but for the spiritual conquest of entire nations as well.

I am completely convinced that ***Successful Leadership Through the Government of Twelve*** has been given by the Spirit of God, as a powerful tool that will help us to effectively accomplish His work. Furthermore it will serve as great encouragement for those who truly feel a call to continue the work initiated by our Lord.

In order to give continuity to His vision, He had to reproduce His character in twelve men. Furthermore, the redemption of the vision would not remain solely with those who were partakers in that era but would continue to this present day. History records how each disciple gave his all in his determination for the vision to continue from generation to generation, until all had a chance to hear the good new of Jesus Christ. In the same way, if we want leadership to last for many generations we should follow the steps of the Master.

If you believe God called you to develop this type of leadership, I am sure that God will give you the grace to develop it and that this book will be an important tool in your endeavor to accomplish all that He purposes for your life.

God can use you to awaken the spirit of those around you. You can help reproduce Christ in each of them and transform them into efficient and uncompromising leaders, until all humanity turns its face to God. God is ultimately the only hope for the spiritual crisis that our world is facing.

PART I

LEADERSHIP & VISION

Chapter One

THE POWER OF A VISION

"A dream is a creative idea from God, revealed to the mind of a man for him to carry out." C.C.D.

DECISIVE FACTOR FOR LEADERSHIP

All effective leadership is associated with a vision. The vision determines everything in the process toward success.

When God called me into the ministry and gave me a dream of having a church as immense as the stars in the heavens and the sands of the ocean, He showed me that each grain of sand represented a person. I then began to understand that He was challenging me to work with souls, to guide them spiritually and helping them find refreshment in Him.

Throughout biblical history, we notice that God, in order to bring about His purpose, chose a man to whom He would reveal His will. He then gave him instructions and guidelines to implement that vision and surrounded him with people who, when identified, would embrace the vision and become the support system and the force that would drive the vision. We see here that there is a direct connection between leadership and the vision.

THE VISION FOR THE NEW MILLENNIUM

All that exists originated in a vision that God had from creation. I believe there has never been a person who has received a vision from God and succeeded in carrying it out without first applying continual perseverance until reaching its fruition.

In order to carry out God's vision we must first experience small victories and fight small battles everyday. As we continue to overcome obstacles we will reach our goals, thus fulfilling our dreams until the vision is complete. It is said that great men who one day forged the destinies of entire nations began with a strong desire to be valued and accepted. Once encouraged, they managed to prevail over all kinds of adversity such as infancy traumas, romantic deceptions, etcetera.

That is why neither rejection, familiar, cultural or economic barriers should be obstacles to prevent us from achieving our God-given dreams. This is the perspective from which the Lord desires that new leaders develop.

The arrival of the year 2000 was filled with so many expectations that could only be met when leadership recognized and learned to live according to God's vision for their lives. The way to work effectively is demonstrated by the Lord in His act of creation, culminating in His masterwork. It is the path that will help us to achieve the work that He has entrusted us.

Let's start from an undeniable and remarkable fact: We are all a product of a vision that God had of us. He diligently thought about the most infinitesimal details that would fit the human being and afterwards proceeded to develop His vision and did not rest until He saw His work completed. This is what Paul refers to when he says, *"For we are His workmanship...*" (Ephesians 2:10). Before God created us and shaped us with His hands, even before He took matter and molded it in the shape of man, He designed us in His mind. *You are the fruit of God's dream.*

We are human beings endowed with qualities, gifts and endless resources that are stored in our minds. In His mind and in His thoughts God projected an image of man before He determined to make him into His image.

Matthew Henry comments, *"If the elaboration of our thoughts is so mysterious, what will we say about the Devine mind, whose concept is such an alive and substantial Word that He is a Divine person? God the Father worked with something that had logic and we were its end, saying, 'Let Us make man in our image, according to our likeness'" (Genesis 1:26).*

Man has the same creative capacity to design, as does God. We as His sons should enter in the same dimension of God's vision, to bring forth the Spiritual kingdom to this natural world. Through faith we enter into the spiritual realm and receive creative ideas from God and bring them into the natural realm with the help of the Holy Spirit.

Let's consider that a vision given by God has various aspects including a healthy motivation, accompanied by purity, which contributes to the social and spiritual welfare of one's community. Therefore, a ministry oriented according to these parameters, will comply with God's purposes. It is important that the leader understands that proper vision does not produce personal praise but praise to our Lord. Every leader who surrenders his life to Christ and is willing to serve must have God's vision in his heart, to achieve His purpose on earth.

When a vision does not come from God, generally it is contaminated with selfishness, greed, pride, jealousy and vengeance. When the vision has as its priority the monetary aspect, then it is not a pure vision from Him because the Lord said that the economic aspect comes as a byproduct of the vision. Renowned leaders who fulfilled great visions never had as a motivation the economic aspect. On the contrary, many of them died in poverty but not until their dreams became reality and their names passed on to greatness.

You may ask, *how do I know God's will for my life?* The answer is simple because all things that we wish for already exist. They are in the spiritual dimension, the dimension of Divine blessing. But it is necessary to enter the supernatural and transport them into the natural realm by taking ownership of them through faith, perseverance, patience and discipline. Then they will become reality in our lives.

French novelist Victor Hugo said, *"there is something more powerful than all armies of the world, and that is an idea whose moment has come."* An idea originating from God is one that inspires and motivates us to undertake great things for Him. Of course, it is the path that encourages others to do the same. It is absurd to think in a leadership realm without a vision. There are small visions and others of great dimension. Nevertheless, when we speak of one who has enjoyed much or little success we soon discover that vision was a key element.

Those who understand the purpose of their calling have managed to transcend the ordinary and conquer that which for others is impossible. Great achievements start with a vision that comes from God. The vision that contributes to the development of humanity and its welfare can only come from Him.

The fulfillment of this vision starts with a small seed that, when falling into good soil, develops until it has the correct form and reaches God's intended purpose.

VISION: MOTIVATIONAL STRENGTH OF GREAT LEADERS

Vision is the motivational strength that has driven great leaders to undertake important and significant works not only for their communities but for their personal and family lives as well. It is the vision that makes us victors. The successful leader recognizes the vision of God for his life and brings to bear all of his strength in fulfilling it.

Triumph starts from the moment man brings into submission his mind and thoughts. Satan knows that if he conquers a man's mind, he enslaves him totally. The Lord wants us to have the mind of Christ.

The apostle Paul said, *"Finally, brethren, whatever things are true, whatever things are noble, whatever things are just, whatever things are pure, whatever things are lovely, whatever things are of good report, if there is any virtue, and if there is anything praiseworthy, meditate on these things."* (Philippians 4:8).

It is the mind where we are bombarded with vain imaginations but also where God's ideas are received. Resentment, vengeance and hatred come from the adversary but all healthy and edifying ideas come from God. Victors have learned to embrace ideas and visions from God in the development of their lives.

God's ideas generally come in quiet times, not in times of turbulence nor when one has a broken heart or a bitter spirit. The Lord takes advantage of these times of peace, to reveal to us the ideas that will make us triumph. There are many examples of men who were sensitive to opportunities like this and as a result their names are written in history. These men are symbols of tenacity because when they received a vision, they struggled to achieve it.

One of the greatest North American entrepreneurs, before he was known as such, used to go to the beach to spend a few days out of the week to meditate. In one of those moments of quietness and while the United stated was going through times of economic depression, a revolutionary idea came to this man; invade the hotel industry by building 40,000 rooms at an economical rate.

After writing down the idea, he worked on fulfilling it and in four years saw his dream come true. That's how the Days Inn hotel chain was born. Days Inn operates throughout the United States. This idea came from God because the entrepreneur was a believer.

Mr. J.C. Penny, owner of the chain of stores named after him and a God-fearing Christian, said, *"Show me a laborer with a vision, and I will show you a man that can change history."* Great achievements come through ordinary people prepared for spiritual things. God's vision is never complicated and that is why the vision He gave us is being adopted throughout the entire world.

THE VISION: A POWER THAT COMES ALIVE

To embrace and fulfill the vision means operating on a spiritual level. In the spiritual realm we're able to control all that we wish to have happen in the natural because we are able to see things with the eyes of faith and call things which are not as if they are. Perhaps you feel as the prophet Ezekiel when he saw the vision of the valley of dry bones and knew that the only way to make a change was by Divine intervention. We all have to face challenges but we should not let ourselves be discouraged by circumstances. On the contrary, we must hear the voice of God, which will bring us hope for our future, for God desires relationship with His servants.

When most of the churches in our nation were small in number, God placed in my heart the challenge to build a big church. I immediately thought about the 120 members I had previously shepherded. Although I tried to increase the numbers of members, it was almost impossible to achieve until I decided to believe God. That is when I began to envision the people as the sands of the sea. It was at that time that I had full confidence in my spirit that I would fulfill it.

Though I felt like Ezekiel, facing a whole valley of dry bones, I could see with my own eyes of faith the miracle that God would create in them. The Lord asked Ezekiel, *"Will these bones live?"* The prophet then replies with uncertainty, *"Lord, you know."* But, the Lord gave the prophet the Divine strategy telling him to, *"Prophesy over these dry bones."*

The prophetic word was the path chosen by God to give life to the dead. Interestingly, God has not changed His mode of operation in that He continues to use these same principles so that we can achieve the miracle of transformation in our lives. When the earth was without form and void, God took that prophetic word and executed the will of God's heart. The prophetic word, prophesied through Ezekiel, was the voice of God's heart expressed through His servant. When the word is given, the spiritual kingdom is activated and the heavenly hosts are at work fulfilling that spoken word.

When God gave me that prophetic word, I was not ministering during that season of my life since I had given up four months earlier. He told me to dream of an immense church. I decided to believe that word and a month thereafter I launched what is known today as the INTERNATIONAL CHARISMATIC MISSION. Starting with 8 people in the living room of our home, everyone knew that we would one day be one of the biggest churches in the world. This small group therefore took ownership of the words God had given me and they continually declared them while being in total agreement with this.

In Ezekiel's case, in order for him to see the miracle of revival, he had to prophesy in part. In a similar way, if we have embraced the vision that God has given us, we're not able to conquer it in the first stage, as God has to take us step by step in the process until it begins to take shape. Armed with this experience, we are thereafter able to help others who wish to develop their own potential.

THE SUCCESSFUL LEADER:
A REPRODUCER OF THE VISION

"Then the Lord answered me and said: Write the vision and make it plain on tablets, that he may run who reads it. For the vision is yet for an appointed time but at the end it will speak, and it will not lie. Though it tarries, wait for it; because it will surely come, it will not tarry."
Habakkuk 2:2-3

What was Jesus' vision? He didn't pretend to become a martyr nor did He pretend to have a multitude of followers, nor did He desire that the world know Him as a great master or a remarkable religious leader. His vision went further, to redeem humanity from damnation and bring salvation to them. Apart from Him was no other hope for man. Paying a high price, He left His throne of glory and splendor and made Himself of no reputation. He took the form of a servant and came in the likeness of man. He humbled Himself and became obedient to the point of death, even the death of the cross on Calvary.

He thus achieved His vision of salvation for all those who would believe Him. Sharing the message of salvation with others should be our responsibility, so that they too might come to know Him. Solomon said, *"Deliver those who are drawn toward death, and hold back those stumbling to the slaughter"* (Proverbs 24:11). Paul says that we are spiritual fathers of those whom we beget into the gospel of Christ. For that reason, we must assume the responsibility to reproduce Jesus' vision in others. This too is an example of successful leadership that is demanded in our time.

Perhaps he prophet Habakkuk makes reference to the vision of the Twelve, which is part of the biblical scheme, that God's servants have used sporadically, in different stages in the history of the church.

From the beginning God established the model of the Twelve and it is through this model that Jesus' vision is reproduced. The master dedicated Himself to disciple others, to center His attention on the Twelve that were selected after a night of praying. In doing this, He established the secret of success to disciple the nations. He applied a process of reproduction that helped propagate the vision. When we see large multitudes we might be overwhelmed at their number. But in order for the vision to take shape it must be developed and nurtured within the context or environment of small groups, which the model of the Twelve is destined to do. In the same way that there are living cells in our body, the Twelve are living cells that are reproducing constantly. Similarly, the church will effectively grow because each member knows to which group he belongs and the goals he must reach.

Being aware of this concept, we have made efforts to reproduce this vision in others and to get each one of our leaders to do the same. A minister in Manus, Brazil decided to adopt our vision and started to proclaim it in his city and in his country. He went to Jerusalem and in one of his sermons described the model of the Twelve. When he finished, a woman approached him and gave him a lapel pin that was a replica of a chest piece of the high priest with twelve stones, and said, *"Pastor, twenty-two years ago I made this lapel pin and the Lord told me that a man will come to preach about the model of the Twelve. When you hear his message, give him the pin because that is my vision and it will be the vision that will impact the nations of the earth."*

That was an emotional moment for the Brazilian minister because God confirmed to him that he was implementing the proper vision. When I went to Sao Paulo to preach, the same preacher approached me and with tears in his eyes, he shared his experience before the church and said to me, *"Pastor Castellanos, God told me that I should formally present you with this lapel pin because it does not belong to me, since the vision was given to you by Him."* On that moment when the lapel pin was presented to me, the place was flooded with the glory of God and the entire church wept. It was an emotional moment that I will always treasure.

More than you can imagine, is possible, when you reproduce the vision that God has given us. Many nations of the world will turn to this vision of the Twelve and will multiply greatly because this is God's strategy for the twenty-first century.

Chapter 2

THIS IS LEADERSHIP

"Yearn to be a winner, make use of all your strength to accomplish the vision and when you have achieved it, you will understand you have only taken the first step on the ladder to success." C.C.D.

THE INFLUENCE THAT ATTRACTS FOLLOWERS

When they asked the great art master, Michelangelo, about his work, The David, he said, *" The image was always there, and all I did was remove some rubble to uncover it."* The same is true with the model of the Twelve. It has always been there, except now the Lord directed us to remove some *rubble* that prevented believers from seeing it clearly.

Giving shape to our beautiful model has taken nearly 10 years to fine tune and all the while, continuing to yield, great sensitivity to the guidance of the Holy Spirit. Contributions from the leadership team have been very valuable. Although God gave me the idea, the team of the leaders has continued to provide valuable input and support from the birthing, to the establishing and the fulfillment of this vision. This is therefore the product of teamwork.

The Lord had to test it first in our own ministry, in order to later inspire other ministries, to hopefully implement this vision I their own ministries. Those who have already adopted this concept have seen their churches, in a short period of time, multiply in membership.

THE IMPORTANCE OF GUIDING OTHERS

One of the greatest challenges that a pastor faces of his members of the community is, to develop them into leaders. The day that development stops, growth in leadership reached a halt. God sends valuable people to each church congregation. Unfortunately, they can easily be distracted with material wealth, greed and a host of other enticements that never satisfy their thirst for more. These distractions remove them from the right path, Christian leadership.

The purpose of leading is to exercise influence on others and to achieve development of their highest potential. This influence involves the molding of character, the discovery of values and the acknowledgement of personal attributes. The true leader is one who leads the individual in the development of his fullest potential. The one learning can in turn influence others in the same positive way. The way in which the Lord exercised His leadership which always consisted of diligently motivating his disciples with the right attitude, so that they would carry out the vision from their hearts. The work that the Lord developed in His twelve was so effective, that they not only declared His doctrine to the whole world but also, joyfully offered their lives for the cause of Christ.

CONTINUAL MOTIVATION

Every successful leader must continually motivate his team. Great corporations that have strong leadership in the marketplace have done so because they have motivated those individuals that make up their basic team.

In the church, the pastor must be the visionary. The vision must descend to the leadership team and in turn, descend

30

toward its members. Thus the pastor must be an ongoing apprentice of the vision so that he may continually teach his disciples. In our case, the existing relationship with the leadership is permanent. Every week we meet, not so much to deal with administrative issues but to motivate, minister and to keep ourselves in faith.

The law of the master teaches, *"If you stop growing today, you stop teaching tomorrow."* A pastor friend of mine used to say, *"Pity me the day I believe that I am a professional in ministry,"* inferring that the blessings would then cease. Apprenticeship is like manna. We need God's rhema word everyday to feed ourselves as well s our disciples.

The concept of influence gives meaning to true leadership. It encourages and motivates the individual. It also motivates him towards innovation, challenging him to discover and utilize his gifts and talents and above all, instructing him until he has the capacity to influence others. Leadership is a cycle of influences. The apostle Paul said, *"Imitate me, just as I also imitate Christ"* (1 Corinthians 11:1). One of the most basic principles I follow is to live my life as an example that others can follow.

COMPELLING PERSONAL DEVELOPMENT

The leader must, at every turn achieve personal development. The vision in turn becomes a key element because the vision is the proper path that should be followed. However, in the process of achieving the vision, success will depend upon the righteousness of the leaders. The basis for which others will have trust in us is integrity in our personal life. Paul admonished Timothy in 2 Timothy 2:15.

"Be diligent to present yourself approved to God, a worker who does not need to be ashamed, rightly dividing the word of truth."

A genuine leader is consistent with what he says and what he does, including influencing others, to the point of achieving change in them. Undoubtedly, this change can be positive or negative, depending on the perspective from which one is leading. Our task is to tilt the balance toward godly principles and values, hence our influence must be positive.

Throughout the sixteen years, I have been leading numerous groups of individuals. We have focused on the personal interests of each individual and on their improvements of their lifestyles. This has been fundamental in achieving excellent dependability within the leadership. People feel guided and led when they make changes for the good in all areas of their lives. They not only take shelter under sound leadership but start training others with the same principles, producing great results as well.

In conclusion, leadership is the job guiding others, exerting positive influences in their lives, recognizing unique aspects in them, while at the same time motivating them to develop plans of action for their personal growth as for others. One who acts as a leader, guide or model tries to motivate those around him to voluntarily target their energies toward fulfilling their desired results.

In our time, much has been said about the leadership crisis. The world yearns for righteous leaders, in families, the children yearn for responsible parents and parents even yearn for their children's respect. Positive influence is desperately needed to give life a righteous path.

FORGE BRAVE ONES

A coward cannot have a school of braves, nor can the brave have a school of cowards. If we want to form brave leaders, the must be taught by brave leaders who are fearless, confident and neither have an inferiority nor superiority complex. Faith and self-control are necessary for the conquest. God's strategy to forge His warriors does not change. He always tests us with small things. God would not give us great responsibilities if He was, not sure that we were able to assume them.

When David was a child, being the youngest, he was entrusted with the task of shepherding a flock of sheep, a task his brothers saw as boring and uneventful. He protected and cared for those sheep as though his life depended on it, shielding them from the dangers of wild beasts and lions. He was always successful. In the insignificant place where David spent many years of his life, God Changed his heart by giving him great courage and strength. Later, when he saw the Philistine giant challenging Israel's army, he had no doubt that he could defeat him. His reasoning *was that if God has delivered him from the bear and the lion, He would deliver him from this great giant also. David* was fearless, that's why when he came face to face with the giant, he told him,

"…You come to me with a sword, with a spear, and with a javelin. But I come to you in the name of the Lord of hosts, the God of the armies of Israel, whom you have defied. This day the Lord will deliver you into my hand, and I will strike you and take your head from you. And this day I will give the carcasses of the camp of the Philistines to the birds of the air and the wild beasts of the earth, that all the earth may know that there is a God in Israel." 1 Samuel 17:45-46

To nurture others with the courage that David demonstrated requires that they receive proper instruction.

The psalmist said, *"...I was made in secret, and skillfully wrought in the lowest parts of the Earth"* (Psalm 139:15). As God worked with us when we were forming in our mother's womb, this is the way that He wants us to be developed so that we train others to reveal Christ to the world. Preparation requires times of quietness during which the Word of God, by power of the Holy Spirit, instructs our spiritual man. Just as immediately prior to giving birth, a baby can no longer remain in his mother's womb but is delivered into the world, God expects the same in the spiritual realm. These basic fundamentals of Christianity pave the way to fulfill the sovereign purposes of God.

Chapter Three

PREPARE FOR SUCCESSFUL LEADERSHIP

"Whoever gives the best of himself to help others, prepares the way and makes it easier for them to achieve success." C.C.D

We all desire success but we must work to achieve it. The apostle Paul said, *"They all run the race, but only one will take the prize."* How many ministries In God's service have truly and courageously accepted their responsibility and have worked to excel? O.S. Marvin said, *"Success is never a donation, it is a conquest."* In other words, there must be effort on our part, which requires maintaining high self-esteem and personal encouragement, in order to achieve it.

Years ago when I began in the ministry many novices began with me. But as the years passed, many of them dropped by the wayside. I realized that the reason they dropped out was because they felt defeated even before starting. Those who persevere are characterized by having a strong optimistic spirit, great enthusiasm and a powerful relationship with God. Success must be developed in all areas of our lives. Some expend all their energies to achieve only certain types of success, whether ministerial, entrepreneurial, political or professional and ignore or put very little time into their home lives. Have you calculated the emotional injuries that occur when home and family structure fall apart? One of our goals is to have the best home environment for our children because it will reflect in all other areas of their lives.

THE LEADER MUST BE A DREAMER

God makes a dreamer come out of a leader. This means that your spiritual eyes are opened and God reveals to you the spiritual world while equipping you with a vision. He will not rest until He sees His work finished in you.

I know that the vision of the Twelve is God's vision for the new millennium. Each individual has access to it and it will play a great role in the development of local churches. Its characteristic allows each member of different communities to be involved in the ministry, accelerating their growth through multiplication. For your dreams to come true, you must dream with that objective and spiritually grasp what you desire by applying the processes that are detailed in the vision.

One of my greatest dreams is to see this vision implemented all over the world and in every church regardless of denomination. When God revealed the vision of the Twelve to me in 1991, freshness and a renewed commitment came to our entire church and we entered into an extraordinary growth of cells and membership. Some members who initially didn't understand the concept made efforts to comprehend it.

Perseverance has resulted in so much fruit that the adversary fears the vision. He tried getting us out of the way in order to weaken the vision or cause it to fade but he didn't consider that, *the man of God is immortal until he has accomplished his purpose on this earth.*

When a leader enters the world of dreams, guided by the Holy Spirit, God can take him to great levels of achievement to carry out the pursuit to which He has called him.

LEARNING TO DREAM

We all have dreams of conquering something that appears impossible. Even if man achieves his personal dream this doesn't produce full happiness because man is never satisfied but always desires more. However, when your dream comes from God it sets you apart from others because you begin to understand the desires of God's heart. In this way, you can start to conquer what might be considered foolish to others.

Some interpret God's dream for their lives by living a life of abstinence, sacrifice or poverty. Others interpret it by serving those less fortunate. But the dream that truly comes from God produces peace, welfare, confidence and happiness. That person always sees the fruit of his efforts and it takes him beyond the ordinary to climb to greater dimensions because he believes and has faith in God. In this way, he projects himself as a successful person while running the risk of being misunderstood by others. He becomes unstoppable by criticism since he is carrying out what God has given him to do. When I knew the desire of God's heart for my life, I understood that He wanted the best for me and it was then that I entered that level of faith that helped me to find my place in the body of Christ.

MAKING OUR DREAMS COME TRUE

Great and noble dreams are the material with which we weave our future. The man who desires success must be as impregnated with a vision as a pregnant woman who, even though she cannot see her child's development, she prepares for what the child will need after he is born. In the same way, when we possess a dream and a vision given from God, we must not let circumstances deter us but should speak about the vision as if we already own it. Our dream should already be a reality inside of us. Our vision must be accompanied by an assurance that it is God's purpose for our lives and this should be evident to others. We must profess it day and night until it feels like a powerful flame burning in our hearts. For example, the vision of our Lord Jesus was to edify His church. To do that, He chose twelve men whom He trained for three-and-a-half-years.

He reproduced His character in each one of them and showed them what it was to have a true encounter with Him. From this aspect, He would ultimately bring about the edification of His Church and spiritual columns that support the Church, His twelve apostles. If we take a closer look at the way the Lord trained His twelve, we find that it is the most effective method in existence, i.e., working intensely on individuals who would later support the mission of Christ.

When a church begins to grow, strategies are required not only for preservation of the church but to assure that each member keeps his own identity. The greatest risk that members are exposed to, is becoming one more head in the crowd.

The power of the vision using the model of the Twelve caused me to see the great blessings found when one develops well-structured leadership through this strategy. In the revelation God gave me, He said, " *If you train twelve men and pour into them all that I have given you and you cause each to reproduce in another twelve, and it is these twelve more, you will be able to look after each individual in the church.*"

Through this model, that we will look at in great detail, in the second part of this book, we have personalized shepherding for the entire membership of the church. At the same time, as we become aware of the different problems people face in the church we are able to help them personally in their situations and minister to them spiritually with God's guidance when necessary.

TOTAL COMMITMENT

Success is the result of one's commitment to God. When God gives a dream, it is our duty to pursue it with all our strength until we see it come to fruition. After God gave me the vision of the principle of the Twelve, I noticed that my mind began to shift into believing it was possible and I began to completely change.

I finally felt that I could really be a pastor of a great church. In the beginning of this new challenge, I was overflowed with God's mercy, devoting an average of 14 hours per day to minister to peoples' needs.

As they found answers to their needs, the news spread fast. Day after day the number of people coming increased and it became necessary for me to double my efforts until I became so exhausted. Through my own ignorance this was my understanding of commitment. Then God showed me that the commitment to His dream I not only hard work but strategic work as well.

When God gives a vision to a man, the mission can only be developed when his leaders strategically involve every member of the church. This motivated me to train people so that they could help me minister. Therefore, anyone who was in need of counseling or in need of prayer could come by the church any day of the week to receive ministry.

Thank God for my leaders in the different ministries because with the 20 believers whom I have trained, I could now do a much better job than I would have been able to do alone.

Although Moses was anointed, he needed a team who could work with his same spirit to provide for the diverse needs of the people. After Moses chose seventy-two righteous men, God took from the spirit in Moses and deposited it within them. In the same fundamental way, God takes from the anointing in the man to whom He has given the vision and reproduces it in the existing leadership, in order for them to reproduce it in others.

If this is properly done one can count on the whole church for being committed to establishing God's kingdom on this earth.

Chapter Four

LEADERSHIP WITH SPECIFIC OBJECTIVES

"Be prepared to assume great responsibilities, because the courageous conquer the mountain summit while cowards die trying to go around it." C.C.D

Ten years ago, I called my brother-in-law Cesar Fajardo and asked him to pray about leading the Youth Ministry at our church. At that time, he was establishing a corporation in the emerald business, which potentially represented vast amounts of revenue.

When we started to talk about his salary, he tried to avoid the subject because what we could compensate him for, would be almost nothing compared to what he would be earning in his new venture. The resulting financial negotiations that were presented to him started sounding better. However, the day that he was going to sign the incorporation documents, the Spirit revealed to him that this was not His purpose for his life, so he firmly responded to his associate, *"I have decided to leave the corporation because I feel that my place is in the church to develop the ministry that God has given me."*

The man was astonished and told him, *"Think about your future, about your family and about your finances because I don't think the church can give you more than you can make with me."* This didn't make sense to his associate but for my brother-in-law it made perfect sense.

I began to realize that true leadership should not focus on the economic welfare of the individual but on the fulfillment of God's purpose for his life.

A few months after my brother-in-law made this decision, the emerald market suffered a crisis and many businessmen lost their capital, including his associate.

Meanwhile, God started to bless the Youth Ministry in a very special way, making it one of the most significant ministries in the year 2000 in North and South America with more than 6,000 cells.

CLARIFY THE PURPOSE

Often we are impressed by services where we observe people responding to alter calls in search of a touch from the Holy Spirit, only to leave the same way they came in. The leader then wonders, *where is the fruit of my work?* This happens when a leadership is without defined objectives or specific goals. God gives us great responsibilities when He is sure that we will be able to assume them.

A pastor I met in Central America told me that about 200,000 people had visited his church in a span of only five years but he had not been able to retain them. In another instance, I met an outstanding leader who is being used by God in his church where they are experiencing manifestations of the Holy Spirit which have turned into revival, like no other Christian organization has experienced in present day Europe. But he testified, " *Approximately 900,000 people have visited us in the last three years and I only have a membership of 1,500 people. My greatest concern is how to retain the fruit. However, about a week ago, the Lord talked to me and said that He would give me the strategy to conserve this harvest of souls He has been giving me, and I think that your arrival to the United Kingdom is God's answer to my concerns."*

This situation is being observed in different ministries worldwide. We cannot fall into complacency unarmored by the impact of monetary success. The vision must have a purpose and the time has come to define it. We must not allow ourselves to be surprised by crowed church services. Be careful, it can become a diversion from the true purpose for which God has called us, His evangelistic mission. If the people are not being fed, we are not doing our duty to transform them into true disciples of Jesus. We are therefore losing sight of our primary objective.

THE IDEAL PURPOSE, TO MAKE THE VISION FLOW

Before departing this world and aware that His mission had to continue and that those who had to accomplish it were His disciples, the Lord Jesus Christ told them, *"All authority has been given to Me in heaven and on earth. Go therefore and make disciples of all nations..."* (Matthew 28:18-19). It's in this statement that God's purpose is thus summarized to the deliverance of all humanity.

The Lord Jesus, as conqueror, admonishes His disciples that they should fear nothing or no one because He is Lord of all in heaven and on earth. We therefore observed biblical leaders who were not frightened by diviners or sorcerers because they knew the secret of spiritual warfare and that every spirit is subject to the power of Jesus.

The apostles knew how to defeat the powers of hell in any city where they preached the gospel. The gospel they preached was charged with power because they had given up all human prejudices and only moved with the leading of the Holy Spirit.

The Disciples', excellent soul winning was not limited by any circumstances. Instead they remained with new believers until they matured and were ready to bear fruit. They knew the true meaning of *discipleship*.

They were conscious of the fact that if they wanted to conquer a city, it would be impossible without first developing leaders. It is not enough that the individual hears the gospel or attends a church. We must develop them into disciples of Jesus Christ, teaching them all things He commanded. Individual follow-up and discipleship guarantees a person's permanent walk in the Christian life and genuine commitment with the Lord.

DEVELOP LEADERS

Developing people is one of the primary tasks to which God entrusted His children. Sons are simply a reflection of what their parents planted in their lives over time. When a son takes the right path and makes sound decisions for his future, his father feels greatly satisfied. He realizes that it was worth all the time that he invested in his son's formative years. Our disciples are like our spiritual sons. They require work, prayer and Divine direction to guide them in the fear of the Lord. The mentor cannot stop until Jesus has been reproduced and formed in them. We should look at our disciples with the eyes of a loving father, looking ahead at what they will become. Just as each son is a treasure that God sends into your home, each disciple is a treasure to enrich the ministry. We should look for the "gold" in them and not at their mistakes. This requires our time and patience. We will see the reward later. In this same way the Lord envisioned the Twelve.

In the ancient Fables of Aesop, there is a message depicting the consequences of a greedy heart. A farmer had a goose that laid a golden egg, morning after morning. He grew rich selling these eggs and as a result he became greedy. Thinking to get all the gold at once, he decided to kill her. To his surprise, when he cut open the goose he found nothing inside.

The same happens to those who try models of church growth programs and when they do not see results in a short period of time, they decide to sacrifice the vision. They spend all of their lives searching for the magical formula that will give them the secret to growth. In our case, the model has worked because each person who comes to our church is received as a blessing from God. We make every effort to give them the right kind of development so that they in turn become a channel of blessing to others. Someone said, *"If you want to plan for a year, sow seeds; if you want to plan for a decade, sow trees; if you want to plan for eternity, sow into people."*

Chapter Five

THE INFLUENCE OF CHARACTER

"Whoever compares himself with those who are under him is mediocre, whoever compares himself with those on his level is a conformist whoever compares himself with those who have some advantage over him is a person with aspirations, but whoever compares himself with those who are on the summit is someone with a leader's heart." C.C.D.

According to the most recent psychological studies, the days in which we live are characterized by the proliferation of neurotic conditions in man. Many people today are in a state of desperation. This is not unusual because according to Luke's gospel our Lord spoke concerning the end times, *"Men's hearts failing them from fear and expectation of those things which are coming on the earth..."(*Luke 21:26).

All of these things are the result of a generation who has tried to develop a life without the fear of God focusing only on material things and leaving their spirits completely empty. That is why men have reached the limit of desperation.

It's a frightening fact that so many "people of success," commit suicide because nothing fulfills them and life makes no sense to them. A man named Fernando was one of those persons. In desperation he paid someone to kill him but the individual returned the money to him and said, *"I can't do that. Go back to your house where your family is waiting for you."*

That same day he tried other ways to commit suicide but was not successful and decided to go back home in the middle of the night. The next day someone invited him to one of our men's ministry meetings and in one of the sessions the speaker said, *"Possibly your name is Fernando and you have been thinking about taking your life because you think that it makes no sense anymore. But let me tell you that your life is precious and that God has preserved it so you can surrender it to His service."* When he listened to those words he was overwhelmed and when we made the call to come to the front, he was one of the first to come and give his life to Jesus. He then asked permission to share his testimony.

I understand now that when a person is weak in character, his accomplishments make no sense. These realities caused me to analyze the transcendental influence that character can exert on an individual who is developing into a leader. Anyone who has a life is filled with God, will reflect it in his character. They become a living testimony of fruit of the Holy Spirit. The leaders that God wants to build up today must be recognized for having a solid character. This is reinforced many times through trials which lead them to have confidence not in one's self but to fully deposit it in God.

GOD MOLDS OUR CHARACTER

Character problems can doom any potential leader and they tend to take us out of the Divine process. In the Bible we find examples of men who had to go through direct dealings with God so that they could fulfill the calling assigned to them. A leader without godly character is as dangerous as a child with a gun.

Moses, one of the greatest leaders of the Old Testament, had to go through years in the desert before God could entrust him with His mission. History records three specific periods of his life:

From birth to 40 years of age: Period of spiritual adolescence.

In this period Moses is conscious of his identity. He knows that although educated in the Pharaoh's palace as part of the royal family, his true people are the people of Israel. In his desire to protect one of his own, he attempts killing an Egyptian with his own hands, acting with human wisdom. Influenced by adolescent impulse he is forced to flee and seek refuge in the desert.

From 40 to 80 years of age: Period of ministerial training.

God allowed Moses to experience diverse kinds of needs in the desert. The change was too harsh when he went from the abundance of the palace to the scarcity of the desert. But this was what God used to decontaminate him from what he had received in Egypt. For each year that Moses was contaminated in Egypt, God used another year to cleanse him. At the same time, God made the most of each day to train him.

From 80 to 120 years of age: Period of ministerial maturity.

"Now the man Moses was very humble, more than all men who were on the face of the earth" (Numbers 12:3) Moses' humility was the result of what God had done with his character during those 40 years in the desert. This is what gave him the strength to endure the grievances of a whole nation, who by refusing to renew their minds never understood what God wanted to do with their lives. Above all, Moses allowed God to use him with signs and wonders,

to such a degree that no man who had ever emerged from Israel, could match. He became the most illustrious man in the Old Testament.

AN INTENSE WORK WITH EACH INDIVIDUAL

Developing true leadership requires intense work deep in the inner sanctum of each individual. It is a work that requires effort and patience to see its fruit and if we do not become discouraged we will achieve extraordinary results.

Because of the type of ministry we have been given, unique doors of opportunity are always open for us to interact with all sorts of individuals. No matter what social status people come from, the first thing we must do is to work on their personal character. As pastors, we wish that these people wouldn't have problems but as a general rule, it's just the opposite. It is similar to duplicating the experience of David.

Because of Saul's jealousy, David had to flee to Adullam's cave, *"...So when his brothers and all his father's house heard it, they went down there to him. And everyone who was in distress, everyone who was in debt, and everyone who was discontented, gathered to him. So he became captain over them. And there were about four hundred men with him"* (1 Samuel 22:1-2).

David spent many years working on the character of these individuals due to their upbringing and backgrounds; they had acquired very bad habits that needed to be changed. But David exercised patience and wisdom with them, gradually shaping them into one of the strongest armies of their time.

They all learned to work together as if they were of one mind. History records that, from that group arose more than thirty of David's mighty men.

If being a pastor is your calling, you must consider that the mighty men you need are within your own church.

Maybe you have not noticed them because they live in hardship, indebtedness or bitterness of spirit. But don't get discouraged, work with them and as the years pass you will see their fruit and be satisfied.

SELF-CONTROL AND DECISION MAKING

We can talk about strong or weak character but it all depends on the level of one's self-control. Self-control is the ability of the individual, to order his life aright. It also involves the ability to control one's emotions in a positive manner when dealing with others, especially with subordinates under our rule. It is about an attitude that defines the personality of an individual, especially of the leader by the Holy Spirit.

Character affects one of the most important responsibilities of the leader, decision making. When an individual is not sure of the role he must carry out in his area of service, he is acting out of weakness of character. Consequently, he is affecting the achievement of the important objectives of the organization for which he is serving.

One of the goals I have set for myself since the Lord imparted this vision to me is to forge leaders with character who will have the capacity to face the challenges that arise on a daily basis. This process was not easy in the beginning and it's still not easy at times. By observing the harvest of thousands of leaders who have studied in our training schools, it is possible to structure the personality of an individual through biblical principles, this way they can achieve a high level of responsibility. This determines and confirms whether we are to be used as instruments of numeric multiplication and spiritual growth.

Let's think for a moment about the 5 smooth stones with which David chose to face the giant. How did they become perfectly smooth? They were, perhaps, too rough in the beginning but God knew that David would need them one day. The stones were made smooth by the river's current in an abrasion process that took years. When they were finally in the hands of David, they did not have any imperfections and were ideal rocks for David's assignment. Therefore, when they were fired, due to their smooth surface, they hit perfectly on the target of the giant's forehead.

The apostle Peter referred to us as living stones, i.e., our character is being formed on the river currents of this world, where we will oftentimes clash with those close to us, such as our own family or with members of our community. We may not understand why they behave the way that they do but God uses each situation to form our character. Those who know, that each adversity they face in life is part of the process in the Divine factory of character-formation, become ideal leaders.

A GOOD GOAL: PERFECTION

The kind of leadership God expects us to walk in can only occur when men and women are willing to have their characters formed by Him with perfection as their goal.

"Therefore, you shall be perfect, just as your Father in heaven is perfect." Matthew 5:48

The Lord would never give us a goal we couldn't achieve. However, the goal that he outlines for us is very important. He does not expect us to achieve close to perfection, He expects us to achieve full perfection. Friend and best-selling author Dr. Derek Prince comments, *"Lets take from mathematics the word 'round' for an example. Something is either round or it isn't. If it is round, then we are dealing with a circle. There is only one kind of circle, even though there are many sizes of it. God, the Father, is the Great Circle that encloses all. Jesus doesn't expect us to be the same size as God, but He does expect us to have His character. You and I can be circles in the small location where He has placed us with apparently trivial duties that are sometimes even boring. It might be as a housewife or as a driver, but right there God wants us to be a perfect circle, perfectly round just like that great circle that encloses the whole universe, God the father."*

The Lord wants His character developed in our lives. It is not easy to reach full maturity in Christ. This requires dedication, consecration, effort and self-denial. This would be practically impossible to achieve without the help of the Holy Spirit, since His presence in our lives must reflect the fruit of the Holy Spirit, *"...love, joy, peace, longsuffering, kindness, goodness, faithfulness, gentleness, self-control..."* (Galatians 5:22-23). This fruit is only reflected in a character controlled by the Holy Spirit.

Chapter Six

THE PROPER ATTITUDE OF A LEADER

"The motivation of man is like a watch, it does not matter the circumstances because it is always working." C.C.D.

Generally, our attitudes tend to be influenced by our circumstances. When you have friendships with those who possess negative attitudes, you are risking the possibility that those attitudes will become a noose around your soul. One king who excelled in personal integrity was Jehoshaphat. But when he befriended King Ahab he almost lost his life. In order to keep a promise, he accompanied him to war, whereupon the adversary surrounded him with the intent to kill him for they thought that he was Ahab. But when he screamed, the enemy realized it was not Ahab and backed away. He then continued his friendship with Ahab's son and formed a partnership that met to God's complete disapproval. For that reason, all ships of that confederation were destroyed at sea.

Attitude decides our behavior when facing circumstances and is closely linked to family environment. Every sportsman must have an attitude of triumph that comes automatically after years of preparation. The recent world champion of formula car racing, Juan Pablo Montoya, did not triumph as a result of good luck. He had the support of his father who was with him throughout his training when he began even as a child. His father always visualized him as a champion in this dangerous sport.

The apostle Paul, who had knowledge of the field of sports, describes the parallel between the sportsmen, who devote their lives to the goal of achieving a medal or a trophy with the spiritual counterpart. The sportsman knows that he may win or lose but must run with the hope of obtaining the prize. In the spiritual field, Paul hinted to the fact that we are already in the Christian race but that does not automatically make us meritorious of the reward, however, if we attempt to finish the race we should finish as winners. We should never allow discouragement to rule over our lives. We should take the lead in this Christian life and never accept second best. Any trophy that a man gets on this earth is temporary but the reward that the apostle speaks of is the crown of life, which God gives to those who love Him.

At the starting line the athlete is focused with a high degree of concentration. Then, there is the attitude after the race is in progress. When the athlete is running and sees others who have taken the lead, he can easily adopt a discouraged attitude and stay back and finish last. But the one who has a triumphant attitude does not look at the circumstances. During the race he just keeps going and does not allow those thoughts to distract him. But there is still another attitude when approaching the finish line. When starting the final sprint, the athlete knows that there are competitors alongside him and it is then that he gets his second wind. Rejuvenated, he says, *"I must defeat them!"* He breathes in deeply that second wind of air and feels that his strength has been renewed.

That process can decide the outcome of the race. Every athlete knows, " *Attitude is the state of nervous and mental disposition, organized through experience, that exerts a dynamic and guiding influence over the answers that an individual give, to objects and situations with which he keeps that relation."* We must understand that that type of attitude is felt from within and expressed by conduct. In other words, we must have that triumphant attitude inside of us, when we start the Christian race and decide that we are going to reach the finish line.

AN OPTIMISTIC ATTITUDE TRANSFORMS THE CIRCUMSTANCES

God placed creative potential in the mind of every human being right from the moment of creation and for that reason He let Adam choose names for every animal. Adam had to use all of his creative potential. In a logical way he dedicated himself to searching for names that would easily identify each animal. Though the task was extensive, he completed it faithfully. Like Adam, we find ourselves, not facing the task of naming 365 animals but facing the challenges of life 365 days every year and we must look for an objective for each one. This is equivalent to naming or prophetically tracing each day's destiny.

CHANGE OF PARADIGMS

Generally, we tend to do routine activity without giving it much thought. Therefore we have acquired behavioral habits that oftentimes are inherited and many of them have become paradigms that trap us. We don't realize we may be inside of a kind of intellectual prison that doesn't allow for any kind of change.

An example would be of Henry Ford. He was one of the greatest entrepreneurs in the automobile manufacturing industry but he refused to change his traditional mass-production model. He reacted violently by destroying the vehicle presented to him as a fully innovative prototype. This behavior showed that he didn't want any kind of change to the paradigm. Another manufacturing company accepted the same model he refused and it became one of the most popular models sold.

Another example would be that of the Swiss. Although they were pioneers of global watch making, the Japanese had them become displaced. They had an opportunity for innovation but feared change because they were known for their precision of timekeeping. The Japanese intervened with an industry of disposable and cheap watches. This is how they overtook the global industry of watch making.

For those who are developing in the ministry, it is fundamental to understand that innovation does not remove us from His Divine will. If we observe creation, we find that absolutely nothing repetitive exists because God made everything ingeniously and beautifully. If technology had advanced through innovation, at best we should have the ability to conquer entire nations for Christ. A concept that has helped strengthen the individual members of the local church has been the popular Sunday school program. Though it was very good and we tried implementing it within our own church, we noticed that most denominations applied it as a general regulation. For us it only worked with the children. God alerted me to this matter and caused me to see that I could reach the same objective with better results if I would only motivate people to attend a cell meeting. Cells could be established in the areas where people assembled, such as in their place of business or in their places of study. Although the actual location was not the issue, we tried to reach the goal of imparting strong fundamental biblical teaching to each one who had decided to live a Christian life. This was a change in our paradigm and as a result we have made the vision of cells a lifestyle in our community.

FACING ADVERSITY

Remember Job, who suffered a terrible crisis when in a brief season he lost his children, servants, wealth and his livestock. Although his test lasted for only a few months, he said, *"Though He slay me, yet will I trust Him"* (Job 13:4-6). Lamentably, in moments of Job's pain, consolers charged him in with negative words and in these moments of confusion he accepted them and in so doing, sinned against God.

After the murder attempt on my life, having suffered five gunshots wounds to my body, I was in a life and death situation for ten days and the medical reports were not favorable. The prognosis was death. But my wife was firm in her faith and with absolute resolve she knew that I would recover and return to my normal life. In a bold act, she decided to seal the negotiation for the purchase of our apartment, which I had negotiated by word a few days prior to the murder attempt. Even though they tried to dissuade her to wait for the outcome of my situation, my wife said, *"I know that my husband will recover and I want to surprise him with this."* Praise God for that triumphant spirit which did not accept bad reports but only accepted and declared what God said in His word.

If Job hadn't passed this test, his knowledge of God would have remained superficial. But the test gave him the opportunity to know God so deeply that toward the end of the test, the Lord revealed Himself to Job convincing him of his spiritual ignorance. This caused him to say, *"I have heard of You by hearing of the ear, but now my eye sees You.*

Therefore I abhor myself, and repent in dust and ashes" (Job 42:5-6). Although in his own opinion, Job considered himself to be a perfect honest and righteous man. He was missing a single element, brokenness. But God used tribulation to humble him. Likewise, we all must go through different kinds of tests that God will use to bring us to a place of brokenness.

The murder attempt on my life not only brought us personally to a lace of brokenness but the whole church experienced a level of brokenness as well. The church entered a period of continuous lamenting, appealing to the Lord for the life of their pastor. Our membership cried out night and day and we couldn't even explain why we had to go through that terrible tribulation. We now understand that our greatest blessing in going through this test was to come to experience a more intimate relationship with Him. This was something we had never walked in before. Obviously during such a test, one feels abandoned and helpless, like the heavens are as brass and that demons are on the attack. When we endured the test victoriously, the blessings came. Our family, leadership and the church acquired an indescribable level of maturity.

FACING NEGATIVISM

Every winner must learn to live not by circumstances but by what God has said in His Word. Witness the great example of Joshua and Caleb, two of the twelve spies sent by Moses to inspect the Promised Land.

Upon returning from their fact-finding mission, the ten remaining spies rendered a negative report stating that in their opinion, they appeared as grasshoppers and that the inhabitants of the land were known for devouring their own people.

But Joshua and Caleb interrupted them declaring, *"If the Lord delights in us, then He will bring us into this land and give it to us, a land which flows with milk and honey. Only do not rebel against the Lord, nor fear the people of the land, for they are our bread; their protection has departed from them, and the Lord is with us. Do not fear them"*
(Numbers 14:8-9)

Because of their secure relationship with God, these two Old Testament patriarchs developed a triumphant spirit, which was also accompanied by a high dose of faith. They did not look at their circumstances nor did they accept the negative report given by the others. Becoming a winner therefore depends upon the way that we form a relationship with God. Every winner knows the power that exists in words. We eat that which comes from the fruit of our lips. When someone continually uses negative language, he binds himself by his own words and the defeat he has confessed will come upon him. Those who have practiced the habit of using the language of faith and confess victory continually, speak those things that are not, as though they are. Otherwise, one becomes prisoner of the words of his lips.

The ten who spoke negatively fell under the judgment of God. Those who allowed themselves to be contaminated with that spirit of grievance and grumbling were left prostrate in the desert, while those who processed with the spirit of faith conquered the Promised Land.

FACING FEAR

We all must face the element of fear. If we allow fear to grow, it will incapacitate us and distract us from God's purpose for our lives. The only way to defeat it is with faith.

We know that both fear and faith have followers and both belong to the spiritual world. Here is the key principle: Faith comes from God and fear comes from the adversary; faith takes us to success while fear leads us to failure; faith produces a positive state of mind while fear produces a negative state of mind; faith makes us winners while fear leads us to defeat; faith brings us joy while fear brings us sadness; finally, faith produces friendship with God while fear brings loneliness.

When my wife Claudia was a little girl, she was attacked and bitten by a dog. As a result, for years she had to fight against a spirit of fear until we managed to identify and expel it. After that experience, the spirit of faith was able to work again in her life and it has motivated her to take amazing steps. For example, she stormed into politics to become a first Christian Senator in Colombia. Never allow fear to deter you from the purpose that God has for you, nor should you accept living with fear simply because it has always existed in your family. The best way to overcome fear is to face it in the power of the Spirit.

"There is no fear in love; but perfect love casts out fear, because fear involves torment. But he who fears has not been made perfect in love." 1 John 4:18

Prominent Scottish historian, Thomas Carlyle said, *"The acts of a man are subservient...until he puts fear under his feet."* When the barriers that fear places before us are overcome, we are ready to develop leadership with clear objectives. One of the most important priorities of a leader is to draw near to God and not to himself. When you aim at a specific goal, for the development of the individuals, who arrive at your local church, you will not see multitudes come in and then disappear from one brief season to the next. On the contrary, our goals will be realized when we see believers strengthened, encouraged and raised up as leaders who will in turn embrace the call to evangelize the world.

A person with character problems oftentimes hides an emotional wound deep in his heart. But when he is open to receive personal or professional help, his weaknesses are transformed into strengths. Fear is one of the most decisive causes of defeat in man and its specific mission is to divert people from their Divine purpose. The thing man fears, becomes a snare to him.

"The fear of man brings him a snare, but whoever trusts in the Lord shall be safe." Proverbs 29:25

A man in his late forties came into my office to talk to me one day. As soon as he sat down he broke out crying. He was a businessman who had tasted success but at that time he was filing bankruptcy. He lost everything and was about to lose his wife too. In his face I could see how defeat had frightened him and fear had become its greatest ally. Through our time of counsel together that day, he began to understand that the antidote for fear was to bring himself and his family in line with the faith of God. After I prayed for him. He left with a new hope and was ready to face adversity, not alone but with the confidence that God was at his side.

FACING STRESS

Some time ago I was surprised to hear from a man who had accomplished extraordinary things in his life and ministry. His work started in his own country and went around the world, indeed a powerful testimony of his faith.

He was Evangelist Benson Idahosa in one year. But God began to tell him that if he maintained that pace of work, He would take him home to glory. Although he was a vigorous man and only the age of thirty-one, stress killed him. His heart couldn't handle the pace of work he was undertaking and he suffered a massive heart attack that took him to the grave. I believe that leaders shouldn't have to face that terrible enemy called stress that comes as a result of excessive work. We should give our bodies the proper rest they need.

Every leader must work strategically without confusing his occupation with productivity. Stress is generally a result of excessive work without due rest or the result of not having a clear vision of what one wants in life. This results in frustration. The clearer one's vision is, the less the risk of sickness. There is a connection between the way that we think and our corresponding behavior because it has been proven that a high percentage of sickness is psychosomatic. Solomon said, *" Just as the thought in his heart, so is he."*

There are a series of negative feelings directly responsible for producing such ailments as fear, terror, aggressiveness, et cetera. These ailments influence the behavior of the individual resulting in hypertension, ulcers, gastritis, asthma and the like. This can be avoided if we maintain a healthy mindset by not entertaining negative thoughts because it is a known fact that accepting one negative thought requires ten positive thoughts to counteract it.

The best way to maintain a healthy mindset is by continually meditating on the Word of God, which will in turn strengthen your faith. That's why the apostle Paul said, *"Let the Word of Christ dwell in you richly in all wisdom"* (Colossians 3:16). He also instructed the church to, *"Put on the whole armor of God that you may be able to resist in the evil day."* Part of the armor is the helmet of salvation, which is used to protect our minds. By keeping our minds saturated in the Word, we build a protective wall against negative darts thrown by the enemy.

For example, the day of the murder attempt on my life as I mentioned earlier, my wife's optimism and mindset were tested. She saw me in a state of agony fighting for my life and responded with authority and serenity grabbing my arm and telling me, *"Cesar don't die!"* (It seemed as though I heard that voice so far away).

Then I heard another voice saying, *"Do you think you will live or die?"* Instantly I shook my head and confessed the verse that I had preached earlier that day, declaring, *"I cannot die because, if the Spirit of Him who raised Jesus from the dead dwells in me, He who raised Christ from the dead will also give life to my mortal body through His Spirit who dwells in me"* (Romans 8:11). After I made that confession, the spirit of life came back to my body even though I was fighting against death for 10 days. My wife didn't speak anything negative or contrary to what she believed, not even for a moment. She had to resist negative thoughts but we believed that a positive mental attitude, the prayers of the saints and of course the Lord's intervention is what brought me through.

Having God's Word fresh in our minds and hearts at the moment of testing resulted in my life being spared. Furthermore, my wife, who guarded her mind from negative thoughts, was the complement for the miracle.

Chapter Seven

THE LEADER IN DIFFICULT TIMES

"Have a proper image of yourself. Do not be placed in subjection to others unreasonably because you risk being crushed, nor should you place yourself above others, because you risk being humiliated. Be yourself and you will have followers who admire you." C.C.D.

Great men and women of God were formed in the fire of adversity. What would you do if you were in the middle of the sea on a small boat that was being shaken by strong waves and fierce winds and although you struggled with all your might to pull yourself to safety, it all seemed in vain? That was the situation in which disciples found themselves according to the gospel account in Matthew 8:23-27. Jesus was on the same boat with them but was neither anguished nor distressed. He was peacefully sleeping as if testing their reaction to adversity.

The experience of the apostles during that moment represents a whole teaching for each one of us, for the development of our character. Those desperate men appealed to their natural abilities as expert sailors, to no avail. Although they were experienced fishermen, apparently after many hours of ineffective work it looked like everything was slipping away. They felt hopeless. The situation was confusing and alarming for them just as it is when we face difficult, even impossible situations. But God allows the crucible of adversity, for character growth in His servants.

FAILURE IN THE HANDS OF GOD

In my first nine years of ministry, the churches I shepherded did not grow over 70 members except the last one. I assumed the pastorate when it had only 30 members and in one year it grew to 120, filling our church capacity. But then I observed how some members did not return. With much effort, I was able to persuade some of them to come back. However, when I had managed to convince two to return, I noticed four others missing. It was like the church had a revolving back door that I had not been able to close. I found myself working in a vicious circle, begging people to come to church to receive God's blessings. This frustrated me so much that I felt that the best thing to do was to quit the ministry and stay with my secular job. After I quit, I prayed this prayer, *"Lord, I will not commit to anything related to ministry unless you speak clearly to me concerning the future of my ministry and I will not go on until You do."* Four months later I received from the Lord one of the most profound messages that I have ever heard which brought such conviction and resolve that I have not been the same.

I began to understand that the churches I shepherded only grew to seventy members because that was the maximum number I could shepherd. I needed God to completely renew my mind to break the barrier in order to receive my increase. He told me, *"Dream of a great church because dreams are the language of My spirit. The church you will shepherd will be as numerous as the stars in the heavens or as the sands of the sea, it will be countless."*

From that day forward I could receive God for greater things and felt that He was being merciful to me, taking my failures and renewing my mind, thus teaching me that all things are conquered in the dimension of faith, not reason.

TENACITY TO ENDURE OPPOSITION

It is important to develop internal strength. This is the strong armor inside people that gives them the capacity to endure any difficult situation. I remember my friend John Garcia, who in his prime, was attacked by a severe kidney disease. He had to endure dialysis three times every week. Due to his critical condition the doctor's prognosis was that he had three months to live. It was impressive to see that in spite of the bad news, he did not weaken, nor was he depressed but he was filled with the spiritual courage and the certainty that he would live longer. The Lord extended His mercy and as the months passed, he was still alive. He became a disciple of my daughter Johanna and was part of her group of Twelve. She used to tell me, *"The life of that man is admirable because even though he goes to his medical appointments and the treatment weakens him, as soon as he leaves his doctor's office, he tends a cell. He continues to witness to people and remains busy in the work of the Lord. He is never depressed or sad. He is always encourages. He is the one who encourages the others."* He received treatment in different clinics but that didn't bother him. Instead, he used each opportunity to share the gospel with his roommates and led many to the Lord. This young man lived three more years leaving an indelible mark in the hearts of many people, thanks to his understanding of the power of tenacity.

I had an opportunity to talk with a successful couple that had been going through one of the most difficult times of their lives. Their son of six years had tragically died in an automobile accident and it left them completely shattered. But what surprised me was the wife's positive attitude. She told me, "In this painful time I prayed to the Lord telling Him, 'God, I thank you for the six years that You have loaned us this precious son we could love, educate and enjoy. Thanks Lord, for those years of so much happiness that he brought to our home. Now that you have embraced him in Your arms, I thank You because I know You are delivering him from something worse.'"

When I heard her talk like that I could sense her tenacity. Her mind was saturated in the Word of God because she had a strong resolve, a firm mindset and godly character. It was as if the words of the psalmist became rhema in the life of this woman: *"You comfort my soul."* She became a great support to encourage her husband who, during that time, made the decision to serve Jesus Christ.

It would be practically impossible to develop that type of tenacity without the strength that God gives us through His Word, which comforts our soul and encourages us to keep going. We acquire tenacity when we learn to give our burdens to the Lord. Our mental image is transformed, from that which in the beginning was weak, into a powerful fortress.

If you picture yourself as a pauper that will be the image you are going to transmit to others. When we acquire the right self-image there is a total change in all aspects of your life because we learn to visualize our possibilities and take action.

What did Peter see in adversity? Imagine the ship moving in the water and in the middle of the storm the winds are roaring, the waves are hitting against the ship and the ship is shaking fiercely. In spite of the odds, in any adversity there is always a possibility of salvation.

The only possibility Peter saw was to appeal to Jesus. This possibility didn't get to him in his first watch or the second or the third. In the fourth watch of the night there appeared a ray of hope, the possibility of change. Many hours elapsed before it came.

The words of Jesus are powerful because they activate the entire invisible realm of the kingdom of God. Jesus said, *"Have courage!"* Peter was afraid and cried out and all the apostles voiced fear. But amid those impossibilities, Jesus said, *"Have courage!"* What is courage? It means to be fearless and keep going.

In 1998 my father-in-law was diagnosed with prostrate cancer. When the test results were in, the doctors noticed that the cancer had spread, affecting other vital organs in his body. Despite this adversity he was impressively courageous.

When he shared the terrible news with all the family, he spoke with absolute certainty that his miracle was already done. Not even for an instant did he show discouragement. Later we prayed together for God to heal him and the Lord showed me a vision in which I saw God's fingers reaching into his body, and removing and pulverizing the cancer. From that moment my father-in-law began to enjoy his health. Later he had new tests done which corroborated the miracle the Lord had done in his body.

The Lord's words are full of confidence. He tells His apostles, *"Don't be afraid!"* Jesus stated these words to the apostles when they were about to perish. Fear is one of the greatest opponents of faith to the believer who is engaged in God's work.

It can become a snare not allowing the believer to advance. But when these fears are defeated with full confidence, we can pursue what God has told us to do. Then we will see His full blessings in our lives.

The Lord told Peter, *"Come!"* This word became a bridge between the vessel and Jesus. And immediately Peter, in an act of faith, started to walk on the water. The power of the Word given by Jesus kept him afloat. Each word expressed by the Lord established a bridge between adversity and himself, If you feel the sea is tempestuous in your life, read the Word because you will find the answer you need. You must begin to walk over your troubled waters without looking to your right or left and whatever God tells you to do, do it.

Peter said, "Lord, I will go!" and although he was walking on His Word, he looked at the circumstances and it was as if he had stepped out of the bridge between himself and the Lord. Looking at the waves and the winds he began to fear and then started sinking, yelling, *"Save me Lord!"*

Anyone who steps out of the path established by God through His Word and looks at his circumstances is exposed to the same risks as Peter. You can drown if God doesn't intervene. While Peter kept his eyes on Jesus he walked on the water, but when he took his eyes off of Him, he became fearful. But the Lord extended His hand and rescued him. Surprised by the apostles' lack of faith, Jesus tells him, *"Why did you doubt me, man of little faith?"*

THE POWER OF PERSISTENCE

"Nothing in the world replaces persistence. Talent does not, because nothing is as common as talented losers. Genius does not, because the acknowledgment of genius is almost proverbial. Education does not, because the world is filled with over-educated people. It seems that persistence and determination will always prevail" **(Ray Froc).**

Persistence must be handled in a strictly positive sense. Persistence always insists on achievement by developing advanced processes. For example, Mr. Jeremy Q. Lyons, president of a typewriter production company had to face the strong market competition of computers. He obstinately continued to manufacture typewriters even though everything pointed to the displacement of such devices. His stubbornness and lack of mental renovation brought him to bankruptcy and turned him into a resentful man filled with hatred towards the computer industry. He became a habitual alcoholic and his family abandoned him. He became vagrant overnight, wandering the streets. One the brink of insanity, a policeman picked him up one morning and took him to the hospital.

There, a friend suggested for him to try what he considered to be the best thing in life. He gave him a Bible, which he read thoroughly until he had a personal encounter with Jesus Christ, whereupon he began the process of renewing his mind. Afterwards, Lyons was hired as a salesman in a computer company. In a short period of time he became one of the most productive salesman, so productive in fact that he was able to open his own distributing company. Shortly thereafter, he opened five more retail outlets. His earnings increased exponentially and he recovered his family. The enemy had consumed his mind, causing him to use persistence in a negative way by insisting on the continued production of typewriters. But the power of God prevailed, penetrating his mind until He turned him into a man of success.

For God to impact a whole nation He doesn't need anyone's genius but simply the disposition of each individual to execute His will. You may have heard the story of an atheist woman who dared to challenge God saying, *"When I die, I want to be buried in a steel vault since I don't believe in the resurrection of the dead. I will show God that he was wrong because this tomb will remain sealed."* When she was buried, someone dropped a seed of a particular plant that fell between the edges of the casket. Some time later the seed, grew into a plant. The plant split open the steel vault, completely exposing the woman's remains. God only needs a willing heart because with one person submitted to His will He will embarrass even the greatest skeptic.

Before he was President of the United States, Abraham Lincoln experienced a chain of failures But these failures, instead of discouraging him and taking him out of action, propelled him to achieve his ultimate purpose. Each of his apparent failures were steps that gradually took him to success:

In 1832 he lost the election to the Senate.

In 1833 he failed in business.

In 1835 his wife died.

In 1836 he suffered a nervous breakdown.

In 1838 he was defeated as a Representative to Congress.

In 1843 he lost the election to be nominated to Congress.

In 1848 he lost for a second time the nomination to Congress.

In 1849 his application to the Registrar's office was denied.

In 1854 he was defeated in the elections to the Senate for the third time.

In 1856 he lost the nomination for Vice-President of the Unite States.

In 1858 he lost the election to Congress.

It wasn't until 1860 that he became President of the United States.

After 28 years of failures he acquired the triumph he so much desired. Lincoln was persistent and only a man of firm character can persevere to the end.

Chapter Eight

THE WINNING LEADER

"Tenacity is an internal strength that helps one endure indescribable pressures. It is similar to internal armor and great leaders are made of this material." C.C.D

Generally, anyone who possesses good leadership skills develops simple plans of action that others may be equivalent to an entire odyssey. A leader must fight great battles if he wishes to attain the purpose for which he is in this world.

THE POWER OF THOUGHT

"For as he thinks in his heart, so is he." Proverbs 23:7

If a computer that could do the functions of the human brain were built, it would occupy a space as big as the tallest building in the world and would be unable to produce a single thought. American philosopher and poet, Ralph Waldo Emerson said, *"What is found on us and around us is totally insignificant compared to what is inside us."* The greatest battle a human being fights is in his own mind. Behind the veil of the visible, the invisible world exists. That is where the adversary deviously plots all kinds of devices trying to conquer the minds of men. Many believe that such thoughts originate from themselves. *"A thought is like a note, you accept it or reject it, depending on the signature"* (Anonymous). Spanish play write, Pedro Calderon de la Barca, so profoundly stated, *"Who could have control over thoughts which are so light and subtle, as they have no body? They trespass the walls, trespass the chests and see into the deepest of one's soul."*

The man who controls his mind will completely control his whole being. Therefore the adversary struggles to control man through his thought life. He presents sin as if it is desirable and bombards him by using all means of communication to subdue him into slavery. *"All thoughts that differentiate us from God, or that don't point us to Him, are barriers in our path"* (Anonymous).

GOD'S THOUGHTS

Everything that you see in the cosmos is the byproduct of thoughts that originated in the mind of God. He first conceived in His mind: flowers, mountains, seas and rivers. He further conceived of fish, jungles and all of the animal species. He not only thought about them but He made them into a reality.

Everything that exists was designed and manufactured with much wisdom and perfection and the fruit of this Divine wisdom was transferred to man so that he could generate ideas in his mind as well.

When we look at the things that man has wrought we can understand that they are not the result of chance but were guided by Divine inspiration. God is the One who gives man witty inventions and every good thing. The bed on which we sleep, the clothes we wear, the house in which we live, the office where we work, et cetera, are all results of ideas inspired by God's superior mind.

The vision therefore does not come from man it comes from God. When a leader finds a way out of a situation and defines solutions after consulting with God, he is acting out of Divine purpose. The Holy Spirit is in charge of taking God's thoughts and placing them in ours so that everything is done according to the Father's plans. God's vision get man out of vain and trivial pursuits and raises him to dignified and honorable positions, driving him to walk the paths of victory and triumph.

A visionary possesses the ability to transform the absurd into something logical, the vile and despicable into something pure and the weak into something strong. When the leader allows him self to be guided by a vision originating from God, the phrase, *"I can't"* disappears from his vocabulary and instead he says,
"I can do all things through Christ who strengthens me."
Philippians 4:13

When a person in leadership accepts that in order for vision to develop it must begin with God, he is open to be an instrument to transform lives. This reality can change nations and continents. This type of leader understands that he is indebted to his fellow man and therefore the best way to return the favor is to develop a vision to win the world to Christ.

THINK AS A WINNER

When the leader renews his mind, he thinks like a winner. The ability to think is the greatest blessing God gave us. Thought is like a fertile field where diligence is required in deciding what to sow in it. We can plant the seeds of truth. They are revealed to us through God's Word or we can let the weeds cover it. *"A negative thought tends to be counteracted by ten positive thoughts"* (Anonymous).

Think like a winner and allow your mind to be completely saturated by God's Word. I reiterate Paul's word, *"Let the word of Christ dwell in you richly in all wisdom"* (Colossians 3:16). God's Word then becomes the purifying spring in our lives and it helps remove all kinds of contamination that penetrates through our senses and impedes our thoughts as God's winning leaders.

Chapter Nine

EFFECTIVE LEADERSHIP

"A visionary possesses the ability to transform the absurd into something beautiful, the vile and despicable into something pure and the weak into something strong."
C.C.D.

God needs leaders with character comparable to His own. David's life was exemplary because God molded him from the time he was young until he reached maturity. He became the model leader of his nation and God further established a perpetual covenant with him and his descendants.

Since his early years, David had a tender heart towards the things of God. His leadership training didn't start when he was King of Israel but he was very young and the forgotten one in the family. He suffered the usual pressures of family life, having experienced rejection from all the members of his family and was required to do all the menial and mundane tasks that his brothers despised. But what made David great was the way that he responded to each situation; he had an obedient heart and was faithful to what his father entrusted him.

His first responsibility was to look after sheep. David had a very clear understanding of leadership. He knew that he had to answer to his father for the sheep under his care. When a wild beast trespassed the barrier where the sheep were grazing, David did not flee but faced the beast and defeated it with his bear hands. The responsibility of carrying out his assignment tasks and doing them well is what made him a great man. David's faithful and overcoming attitude was admirable. He always strengthened himself in the Lord and never allowed fear to rule his life. In the same way, God tests us with small matters, such as running a family group or some community administrative department so that He can give us a greater responsibility later. And as we perform well in these areas, He will entrust us with more.

David knew the secret of persistence. Success must be the result of a positive mental attitude. If you allow a poor attitude to remain in your mind your results will be poor. What does mediocrity produce? Mediocre results.

What does a faithful attitude produce? Victorious results. We have to guard our mind like nothing else in the world. Paul said we should put on the helmet of salvation. The function of a helmet is to protect the head and this is its equivalent. The importance of saturating yourself in the Word cannot be overstated. The Word must dwell in you beyond measure. When we saturate our minds with the knowledge of the Scriptures, we fill ourselves with positive thoughts and also with a conquering mindset because the Word of God doesn't allow for negativism. All that emanated from the Word is peace and hope.

From David's point of view, it was illogical that anyone around him should be in fear because he had the mind of the Lord. This made him different from the others. That's why he wasn't afraid to face the giant, as he had already developed himself while in the school of the Lord, amid loneliness and wild beasts. That is where he acquired the courage of a winner. Without a doubt, anyone who aspires to leadership should consider the example of King David.

This ideal is possible when the secrets of effective leadership are discovered and are put into practice, having God's vision as our personal guide.

LEADERS ARE NOT BORN AS SUCH, THEY ARE MADE

"A wise man is strong, yes, a man of knowledge increases strength" (Proverbs 24:5) Strength and vigor are qualities that distinguish a wise leader. These are acquired through a process of character development where one is ultimately able to influence others. He is person chosen to carry out a leadership role regardless of his personality, should be molded by the Lord and guided by biblical principles. That person will be able to influence and motivate others. In order to achieve the ability to motivate others a special internal strength is necessary.

If you want to become a leader you must consider 5 important principles:

All things work together for good. We all go through different kinds of tests and trials throughout our lives, both painful ones as well as ones that have filled us with joy and satisfaction. All have served a purpose in the process of strengthening our character. Young David's experiences delivering his sheep from the wild beasts helped him build strong character with which he later faced the Philistine giant, resulting in victory for the people of Israel. The more adversities you face in life, the stronger the internal force will develop.

There are no losers. Remember that great leaders of human history were forged in times of crisis. Abraham Lincoln made several attempts to reach a position of political responsibility in his country and failed for many years. A journalist paid him a visit. He asked him, *"Aren't you tired of failing?"* To which he replied, *"I haven't failed yet, I just haven't attained the desired results."* And we know that he kept struggling until he achieved success. In the same way, whoever is training to be a leader must try and even try again until he achieves his goals. Small failures must be seen as experiences that will take us to success. Failure waits for those who haven't learned to count on God's direction in their lives. Those who allow themselves to be directed by God are destined for success.

It is necessary to assume responsibility. The ability to assume responsibility is what gives the greatest internal strength to a person. When someone assumes responsibility he is showing signs of maturity, if a person is committed to the vision of the church, he shows a degree of maturity when he prepares, for example, to lead a cell. This way he begins to take shape as a leader. When one takes steps of faith, a powerful strength develops from within him.

Absolute commitment. Commitment shows dedication and consecration to the cause that drives us to leadership and our cause is Christ. The vision we develop can only be lived and experienced, when we involve ourselves in it, not with sixty or eighty percent but are dedicated one hundred percent. If our dedication is mediocre we will not see the results of multiplication. The fruit of abundance waits for the one who fully devotes himself to the mission.

Defining short and long-term goals. God wants each of us to plan our lives and our ministries. This means that we must plan short and long-term goals to help define a specific purpose in life. Our purpose is the goal towards which we work and this is associated with God's dream for each of us. Goals are the bricks with which purposes are built and they define the fulfillment of man. A true leader always knows where he is going in life. Think for a moment of how you would like to be remembered after you die, and why. The achievements you attain will influence the memory and image that people will have of you. Abraham Lincoln, for example is remembered as the great reformer who established social justice in North America. Goals will determine your image in the present as well as the future. Goals are the confessions of faith that allow us to achieve great things.

REPRODUCING IN OTHERS

I had the opportunity to meet one of the most successful artists of our present day. When I asked him if he had won any awards for his artwork, he replied affirmatively. He had won all kinds of awards and gained notoriety in his field.

I then asked him who his successor would be. He then replied, "I don't have a successor." No doubt this artist has exerted tremendous influence over many people. But, it's one thing to influence people through art and it's another to exert influence over faithful disciples who can perpetuate a godly work to future generations.

We must be conscious of the need to forge successors. The spiritual awakening that is near, in these last days, demands the need for a new generation of competent leaders. It is this type of leadership that can influence those who are continually joining the church and showing an interest in taking God's message to others. It is a chain that lengthens where each link represents a committed leader.

When leadership reaches the level of required each person must approach commitment, it will have the ability to shape others so that they reproduce what God has placed inside them. Commitment is acquired gradually but from the beginning, each person must approach and maintain the highest level of service, attitude and performance. It is necessary to equip those who are learning so that they can replace us at any given moment. Also, it is vital that they will have gained the permanent knowledge and maturity for continued growth in their lives. Need creates a team committed to the vision and a reason that drives us to work. Having a committed team is possible if we are seen as an example. People will do what they see their leader doing. They will do as he does and fight for results in the same way.

In genuine and effective leadership, the most important thing is that the vision receives the highest priority and that it followed by expending more effort than is required. What would be worse would be if the time would come, when our strength will not be enough and everything will stagnate because successors have not been developed to carry on with the task.

Let's remember that Paul said, *"Imitate me, just as I also imitate Christ"* (1 Corinthians 11:1). This means that an important step required to have a committed team is to give paradigms of conduct, where the leader becomes the example worthy of imitation.

People will be more inclined to follow a leader who works through the process of ministerial development alongside them. The true leader, worthy of being imitated is the one who instead of saying, *"Go"* says, *"Let's go."*

A LASTING LEADERSHIP

An effective leader endures, along with his followers, who have been formed to perpetuate the work that God has assigned. None of the members of our leadership team were chosen out of sympathy. Each one made an effort and overcame his difficulties. True leadership is not given by one's position or authoritarian rank, as is often the case in our society. Titles tend to substitute for the most important thing, which is the ability to lead others and to bring out of each their best potential. This is not about showing who has more power or authority. True leadership allows us to retain followers of our ideals and our actions. It is absurd for someone to proclaim himself as a leader when no one is following him. As leading author, Rev. John Maxwell, said, *"The most important asset is people."*

Leadership is fundamentally about influence and the target of that influence is " *people."* I therefore decided from the start to guide the bow of the ship the Lord had given me and steer it towards a good working model that my people can follow. This would serve as an example and their development would extend to other levels of influence as well. Success of this newly begun task would depend upon preparation of leaders. These students would possess a vision to win and strengthen disciples in order for them to send their disciples to a field of action with defined objectives. To talk about success and leadership and the ability to duplicate themselves in others, would be futile. The number of disciples that a pastor is training for leadership determines how his success is measured.

Chapter Ten

VICTORIOUS LEADERSHIP

"You possess the most precious treasure; intelligence. Protect it in the vault of truth, accompany it with wisdom, flourish it with generosity and enlarge it with integrity."
C.C.D

An effective tool in our development as leaders is achieving planned goals. Only then can we talk about victorious leadership because the results will have proven it. What we've sown in the past, we will harvest in the future:

When you sow an action, you harvest a habit.

When you sow a habit, you harvest character.

When you sow character you harvest destiny (smile).

"But this I say: he who sows sparingly will also reap sparingly, and he who sows bountifully will also reap bountifully...Now may he who supplies seed to the sower, and bread for food, supply and multiply the seed you have sown, and increase the fruits of your righteousness."
2 Corinthians 9:6,10

When the apostle Paul talked about sowing and reaping, he was taking about spiritual principles that control prosperity. God wants prosperity for His people and in the Bible there are more than 600 verses that deal with prosperity and provision. It is important for us to understand that faith can cause us to prosper. Great technological advances started with an idea that was in fact a Divine seed sown into a man's mind. This allowed man to take great steps until he achieved his objective. A great example of this is Henry Ford's dream of each American possessing a car. This dream could have only come from God's heart. Human beings tend to be egotistic and selfish because while man seems to be doing well, he oftentimes doesn't care what is going on around him. Someone concerned that his fellow citizen is able to own a car is thinking a generous thought. God honored this noble dream and allowed Ford to go down in history as the businessman of the century.

Let's sow good things that come from noble dreams so that we will see the rewards in our descendants. Trusting in people is a virtue that stands out in any good leader, Henry Ford said, *"If my buildings were destroyed or my factories consumed by fire, and I were left only with people, I would build my company again."* Many pastors continually ask me, *"Aren't you afraid that your people could divide your church?"*

I have learned that people feel very stimulated when they are trusted. This entire ministry is based on trusting God and our people.

I am impressed by the creative power in our team members. Many great ideas didn't come from great intellectuals but from simple people. There was a hotel company brainstorming with its team of advisors on how to install an elevator system inside a hotel building. After many weeks of study they concluded that they had to destroy some of the existing hotel rooms to make space for the much needed elevator. Suddenly, one of the entrepreneurs decided to listen to the opinion of one of the laborers on the job site, for what alternative he could offer for that need?

To that question the man answered, *"The truth is that I don't understand why you are always trying to make things more complicated than they have to be, when the solution to this is so simple. All you have to do is build the elevator outside the building facing the street. You could make it glass to enhance the hotel and that way you wouldn't have to destroy anything already built."* That simple idea, which did not come from someone "gifted", originated a whole new innovation in modern building construction. It is important to learn how to listen to our people because they are the ones in permanent contact with others and they know the needs of the community. If we listen to them we may be astonished at what they are able to accomplish.

An outstanding quality for a great leader is to be surrounded with the experts. American industrialist and philanthropist, Andrew Carnegie said, *"I want my epitaph to read: Here lays a man who knew to be surrounded by people who knew more than him."* Generally a leader on a scale of 1-10, who places oneself at 9, will always try to surround himself with people who are on his level. One of the qualities of King David was that even though at the beginning he did not surround himself with brilliant people, he taught them how to be courageous and as a result they were later prepared to give their lives to protect their king.

When Andrew Carnegie was asked what he had done for more that 40 millionaires to be sitting around him, he said, *"Well, when they met, they were not millionaires, I made them millionaires."*

WE TRIUMPH BECAUSE
WE ARE GOD'S MASTERWORK

"For we are His workmanship, created in Christ Jesus for good works, which God prepared beforehand that we should walk in them." (Ephesians 2:10)

In the work titled, <u>The Portrait of Dorian Gray</u>, the author describes the way in which the human being struggles to maintain a beautiful appearance. In this fictional story, young Dorian Gray gasped at his own youth and beauty in a finished portrait of himself. He wished that the picture might grow old while he would remain forever young. In this fantasy, his actual life was represented in the portrait and it was continually being disfigured, since for each bad deed, a wrinkle appeared on the portrait until it completely aged over time. In actual appearance he continued to be a vigorous, handsome young man. It's an interesting fantasy.

Adversity may add wrinkles to your life but generally the purpose of adversity is to contribute to the development of your character. The purpose of temptation is to seduce man to the pleasures of life, destroying him eternally. Pitifully, many live a double life and inside their souls are in anguish.

An unregenerate man acts as a self-tyrant as if he hates himself and would like to self-destruct. How many people have reached the point where they have allowed life's cares to weigh them down and crush them and have no strength to keep fighting, whereupon they find themselves totally hopeless? To lose hope means death because only the dead are hopeless.

The Scriptures say, *"But for him who is joined to all the living there is hope"* (Ecclesiastes 9:4).

When God created man, He did not create him to be a bitter, unfortunate and ruined person. God sent His son Jesus to give man life and to have it more abundantly.

I heard the story of a preacher who was preparing a Sunday message the night before the service. His son approached him asking to play with him. Thinking about how to distract his son while he finished his Sunday message, the preacher quickly took the page of a magazine that featured a map of the globe. He divided it up in several pieces and gave them to the child to rearrange correctly, telling him that when he finished that task, they could play together. He believed this would keep him occupied for some time. But he was surprised when in just a few minutes later his son had finished the task. Astonished, the preacher asked him, *"How did you do it so quickly?"* His son answered, *"It was easy. On the other side of the page was the face of a man. I saw that it was easier to work with the man's face and when I finished, it would give me the world on the other side."*

From that experience came the message that the father preached. It is so important for us to understand that if we maintain a correct self-image, our world will be restored.

A correct image is the result of a balanced life and this comes when man understands that we were made in God's image and likeness.

When God created us, He put His likeness in us. But Satan took advantage of our human weakness to seduce us and lead us down the wrong path. In this way, he pretended to distort man's eternal image.

If Satan could manage to deteriorate God's image in man, then man would have no spiritual support to anchor himself. Satan would therefore be able to control man through the appetites and desires of the flesh. The prophet Isaiah presents us with a glimpse of mankind when he says, "From the sole of the foot even to the head, there is no soundness in it, but wounds and bruises and putrefying sores; they have not been closed or bound up..." (Isaiah 1:6). But Jesus came to take that deteriorated image and accepted the punishment deserved by mankind so that God's image could be restored inside each one of us.

We are the result of a thoughtful and well-designed plan developed in God's pre-established time. God granted us the most precious treasures of all, intelligence and the ability to generate ideas. These Divine attributes allowed us to take dominion over all His creation. This intelligence must be fed by continually going to the main source of inspiration, God's Word. God imprinted His own image in us, thus:

"By which have been given to us exceedingly great and precious promises, that through these you may be partakers of the divine nature, having escaped the corruption that is in the world through lust."
2 Peter 1:4

Peter gives a surety that all which makes up this life and its Divine mercy, have been given to us by the power of God. Therefore, the fundamental requirement we must fulfill is to take possession of His promises, which will help us in our spiritual development until we reflect His image in our character.

Chapter Eleven

CHARACTERISTICS OF A SUCCESSFUL LEADER

"What makes a great man is not his triumphs, but the failure that he has lived through, his tenacity, and his conquering faith before achieving success." C.C.D.

THE LEADER, AN EMOTIONAL MAN

"The spirit of a man will sustain him in sickness, but who can bear a broken spirit?" (Proverbs 18:14)

One day we were celebrating a joyous occasion with a group of leaders in a luxurious club in the city. While we chatted, I perceived an emotional void in some of them. So I requested a private lounge to have some ministry time with the group; 24 men were in attendance. When I started to talk about God's paternal love, I noticed the anticipation in them for me to finish talking and to begin praying for them. I wasn't praying for two minutes, when one of them, known for his quiet and reserved demeanor, started to cry in an unusual manner and then an atmosphere saturated with God's glory, took hold of us that none of them could stop crying. This was a very uncommon sight. We are used to seeing men laugh, yell, clap and shout loudly for their favorite sports team. But to see the way this group was crying was uncommon. At that precise moment two waiters came in the room to serve us coffee and were so impressed with what was happening to us that they left the room crying too. Later, one of them expressed his desire to join one of our cell groups.

When the crying stopped one of them wanted to share the experience he was having at that time. He commented, *"When I graduated from high school, I was recognized as the best graduate of the school. When I received my diploma, there was profound sadness in my heart because the person whom I most wanted to be there wasn't there, my father. He had left my house two years earlier. I remember I crossed the hallway crying because I had no father with whom to share my success. Today, when I came to understand God's paternal love, I found myself in that same place, reliving that incident, only this time I wasn't alone. I could see my Father God, sitting in the audience waiting for me. I saw myself receiving my diploma. Filled with emotion, knowing that my Father was there waiting and that I could offer the achievement to Him, I went down the stairs quickly, and saw how my Father stood up from His chair, came forward and hugged me, saying, 'Son I congratulate you, and let Me tell you that I am proud of you.' That's why I was crying, because I understood that I am important to someone, especially to my Father God."*

When God designed man, He designed him with an ability to give and receive love. Every child is born into this world with a great desire to receive love, affection, warmth, tenderness and protection, among other things.

That's why when a child is hurt; those wounds go straight to his soul. In the first years of life, his emotions are very fresh and new, and any hurt, no matter how small and insignificant, will become an indelible mark in his life.

Even as the years go by, the mark will remain latent in the soul. The strongest wounds a human being can experience are centered in his soul. They are deeper than those experienced in the conscious mind, even though in most cases they are not registered in the memory. In order to experience God's full blessings emotionally, it is important that you periodically stop along the way, and if you have been offended, forgive those who have rejected you or have deeply wounded your heart. Anyone aspiring to leadership must have a healed heart. We have a mirror of history to gaze into of men who have achieved outstanding success in world leadership, while at the same time were controlled by hate. Hitler couldn't forgive the Jewish people and instead attempted to exterminate them. He went down in history as the most evil man of the century. *"To hate someone is to give him too much importance"* (Anonymous) or, as English writer politician, Lord Chesterfield said, *"People hate whoever makes them feel their own inferiority."*

Let's remember that if we are not able to forgive men their offenses, then our Heavenly Father will not forgive our offenses. To receive healing in our heart, it is imperative to do the following:

Renounce all resentment: Don't let feelings of hate, resentment or ill will dwell in your heart; they are the culprits that will produce bitterness in you.

Forgive yourself: Do not let your thoughts accuse you or the mistakes from your past condemn you. We must understand that there is no condemnation for those who are in Christ Jesus. And if He doesn't condemn us, neither should we condemn ourselves.

Forgiveness is a decision: No one feels like forgiving, but forgiveness must be a decision of our will.

Forgiving when accompanied by faith produces healing. Twenty days after I was released from the hospital following the murder attempt on my life, I was having difficulty concentrating in prayer, until one day I asked the Lord what was happening in my life. The answer that came to me was, *"Have you forgiven the men who tried to take your life?"* I understood that resentment was still alive inside of me, so I decided to forgive them, and I prayed this prayer: *"Lord, I forgive with all my heart all those who were instrumental in the attempted murder of my life, and I bless them. Lord, I ask that this murder they planned against me be what You use to save them."* When I finished praying I felt all the weight inside of me, lifted. The resentment disappeared and I felt normal again. I know it is a great blessing to forgive with all of your heart.

A PERSON OF FAITH, FILLED WITH VIRTUE

What comes from above is eternal because it emanates from God and His presence fills the heavens as well as the earth. Just as the heavens are above the earth, so are God's thoughts above ours.

Just before ascending to the heavens, the Lord Jesus assembled His disciples and told them, *"Receive the Spirit."* This same opportunity is for us today, but only the faithful in Christ can receive the Holy Spirit. Unfaithful people are always living under their circumstances and leaning on human logic. It is therefore difficult for them to learn to depend upon God. The faithful leader continues toward a particular objective, overcoming his circumstances and knowing God's thoughts and acting according to what He has commanded. Faith always rises above circumstances because it comes from above. Faith called things that are not as though they are, and is what helps us conquer the impossible.

Faith and virtue go hand-in hand. Paul said, *"Add to your faith, virtue."* The word, "virtue" comes from the Greek "arête and refers to excellence. The "arête" of an athlete is reflected in his post preparation performance. Paul told the Corinthians, *"You are the seal of my apostleship."*

The Corinthians were so contaminated by worldly influences that in order for Paul to have brought about major changes in them, it required faith and virtue. He had to continually deal with their mediocrity and spiritual lukewarm ness. He was a living message to them of unwavering commitment and dedication. It is said about an excellent violinist, who after presenting a recital, was approached by a girl who told him, *"I would give my life to play the violin as you do."* The musician answered, *"Excellence is achieved as fruit of a life of faith, effort, discipline, dedication and perseverance. Faith is the support required to achieve a virtuous life."*

SOMEONE WHO ACQUIRES KNOWLEDGE

To virtue you must add knowledge. God said, *"My people are destroyed for lack of knowledge…"* (Hosea 4:6). We can know many things, but whoever ignores the Word of God will be lost forever. Knowledge of the Scriptures is what guarantees man success. Knowledge of the Scriptures is what guarantees man success and happiness. This knowledge must come as a result of a continual relationship with God, since only He can open our understanding of the Scriptures to us. This demands times of quietness and meditating on the Word of God. In these moments God's Spirit ministers to our spirit, teaching and instructing us in all truth. The Holy Spirit is the only One who knows even the most intimate things about God. Job said, *"The things I did not understand, I investigated."*

In the Christian life we have two goals: first to develop the external and second to develop the internal. The external goal is what we can do for God and the internal is what we are in God.

For many people, being busy doing God's work is a great justification for neglecting their relationship with Him. When we believe in God and have an intimate relationship with Him it will be reflected in our work. From another perspective, it is important that the leader keeps updated concerning what is happening around him. This is a good way to positively influence others. The apostle Paul admonished Timothy, *"Till I come, give attention to reading, to exhortation, to doctrine. Do not neglect the gift that is in you, which was given to you by prophecy with the laying on of hands of the hands of the eldership. Meditate upon these things; give yourself entirely to them, that your progress may be evident to all"* (1 Timothy 4:13-15).

Reading good books is crucial. Educate yourself through experiences of others who have achieved success in their lives. You can then be equipped to teach others. We have a great responsibility to the world and our knowledge must be up-to-date with the demands of a changing society.

SELF-CONTROL

The life of a man is comparable to that of a spirited horse. It's full of emotions, passions and desires that must be controlled through an internal force called self-control. The person with self-control learns to say, "no." He doesn't allow the disorderly desires of the flesh to seduce him. His interior force helps him to put the brakes on carnal impulses. This crucial element is considered an administrator of one's life. Anyone developing in any kind of leadership must be vigilant not to allow small indiscretions that can lead him to destruction. "He who is slow to anger is better than the mighty, and he who rules his spirit than he who takes the city" (Proverbs 16:32). One of these aspects our ministry keeps zealously guarded is the integrity of our disciples. If we teach them to control their impulses they can minister more freely.

COMPASSION WITH FRATERNAL AFFECTION

Compassion is equivalent to permanently living in God's presence. Whenever we go the atmosphere of the presence of God should be displayed in our lives because of the aroma of compassion. We can only achieve compassion in God, not in ourselves. Jesus told the rich young man, *"Why do you call me kind, don't you know the only kind one is God?"* The state of kindness can only be achieved in God.

Fraternal affection must be added to compassion and this consists of expressing love to our brothers. Fraternal love is expressive: if our brother cries, we cry with him. When someone goes through a test, we should identify with his pain and his need and then deal with the matter as if it were ours. This is about mutual support, developed by the will to serve and bless others. When we have friends they will come to be our support in difficult times. That's why the writer of Proverbs said, *"Friends more united than brothers there are."*

Fraternal affection allows us to show that we are an expression of God's eternal love, which requires having a forgiving spirit. When someone accumulates resentment, not only is he affecting his life but his family's life as well.

DEMOLISHING ARGUMENTS

"...For this purpose the Son of God was manifested, that he might destroy the works of the devil." John 3:8

We must understand that in the invisible realm, there are spiritual forces battling against us. Satan is looking for any argument to use against us so that he may go before God and justify his control over us. Every sin committed by man is registered in the invisible world and becomes an argument that allows demons to have influence over our lives. We must have the great example of David to reflect upon. We know that David was a king of Israel and there wasn't another man like him. He was loved by the Lord and was a man after God's heart and he was the sweet psalmist of Israel. One day he sinned by desiring the wife of Uriah the Hittite. After he was intimate with her he sent Uriah to the front lines of battle to be killed. Although it was a secret sin, Satan, who with his demonic legions went before God and aggressively blasphemed his name. David did not know what was going on in the spiritual realm. But Satan brought accusations before God to attack him financially, spiritually and sexually and unleashed a spirit of violence that affected his whole family. Scripture says that the sword never left his house.

Many people are ignorant of the fact that sin by itself brings damnation. Solomon said in Proverbs 26:2, *"...So a curse without cause shall not alight."* There is always something that initiates ill will. Some people say, *"I cannot explain why I am going through financial hardship, why is there dissension and strife in my family or why has violence controlled my family members, bringing moral decline in my home."* Generally, sins from the past mark the way for your future and the only way to cleanse all past sins is to realize that all those arguments were cancelled by the redemptive work of Jesus Christ on Calvary. When Jesus died on the cross He took our place and His death replaced ours. When we believe this, all arguments from the past immediately disappear. That's when the demonic powers have nothing left to hold onto and one's life becomes completely released in all areas of life, family, community and nations.

I was praying for a woman who came to me because she and her family were having financial problems and couldn't understand the reason why. When I asked the Lord to bless her and help her with her finances, the Holy Spirit showed me what was happening in the spiritual realm. I saw Satan presenting an accusation against her before God. I saw the sin she had committed and Satan was asking God for three things in her life for that sin: To destroy her life, the lives of her husband and children and for their finances to be ruined. The Lord said, *" The only thing that I allow you to touch and only for a short period of time is their finances."* I told the woman, *"Your problem is simpler than you can imagine."* When I told her what God had showed me she was surprised and said, *"I now understand why my son had an accident a few days ago and he was unharmed. It was because God was compassionate and merciful."* Paul said, *"...having wiped out the handwriting of requirements that was against us, which was contrary to us. And He has taken it out of the way, having nailed it to the cross"* (Colossians 2:14).

I know the day will come when men will cry out in repentance for their sins just as a father cries for his first-born son who has died. Painfully, that is why Joel says, *"'Now, therefore,' Says the Lord, ' Turn to me with all your hear, with fasting and weeping and mourning.' So rend your heart, and not your garments; return to the Lord your God, for he is gracious and merciful, slow to anger, and great kindness; and relents from doing harm"* (Joel 2:12-13).

In spite of our mistakes, each failure is a step that takes us closer to success. There are many ministries that have passed through desert experiences, especially in the first years of their formation. Solomon said, *"The end of matter is better than its beginning."* All enterprises that managed to get to the top, first had to go through many failures.

"Failure teaches us more wisdom than does success. Usually we discover what's going well before we find out what's going wrong; and probably, he who never makes a mistake will never achieve any discovery" (Scottish writer and social reformer, S. Smiles).

CHARACTER CONTROLLED BY GOD'S SPIRIT

"I say then, walk in the Spirit, and you shall not fulfill the lust of the flesh." Galatians 5:16

There is a great danger I have seen in the last few years in which the gifts of the Holy Spirit are working in people without character and who have not yet developed or formed by the same Spirit. As explained previously, this is as dangerous as entrusting a weapon to a child, and could cause great chaos. We know of the horrible tragedies that were caused by adolescence in different schools in the United States in recent years.

The same thing happens when one who lacks firm character functions in the gifts of the Spirit. For this reason, the Scriptures emphasize the importance of a life characterized by the fruit of the Holy Spirit. We must understand that the gifts that God gives us are favors so that we can enlarge His work. But there will come a day when these will cease and the only thing of value will be the fruit of the Holy Spirit. *"When I was a child, I spoke as a child, I understood as a child, I thought as a child; but when I became a man, I put away childish things"*. (1 Corinthians 13:11).

Think of yourself for a moment as a soccer player who is participating in a World Cup. The television media is covering the event, and the whole world is watching every move the players make, as well as their attitudes and reactions in the contest. We can appreciate the talent of some. But some players lack character, and what we cannot see sitting in the stadium bleachers, is captured on camera. The zoom of the camera shows their talent as well as their character. The apostle Paul said, *"We are spectacle for the world, for God and for the angels"*. He is also referring to the fallen angels.

We can view the world as a stadium, and we who know Jesus, are the players. Among he spectators watching are those who support us and those who are against us. On one side is the Lord with His angels, but on the other is Satan with his demons. Every mistake that we make, the adversary tries to use against us with the intention of removing us from the competition. But the Lord takes our good deeds to counteract the attack of the enemy. In the same way the referee must remove a player from the field, "showing him the red card," The enemy wants to do the same to those who do not have control over their basic character, or flesh. That's why Paul commented, *"...lest when I have preached to others, I myself should become disqualified"* (1Corinthains 9:27).

We must understand that some players on the opposite team provoke those on our team so that they will foul out. When someone possesses self-control and doesn't react violently he demonstrates patience and faith that encourage him to persevere to the end.

Chapter Twelve

STEPS TO ACHIEVE SUCCESS

"A balanced walk consists of putting God first in your personal life, taking care of your body as the temple of the Holy Spirit, having an exemplary family, and exalting God's work". C.C.D

Success is equivalent to achieved goals, dreams and acclaimed triumphs. Success is desired by youth, adults and even by children. Rejection, adversity, family opposition, social crisis or economic pressures should not keep us from achieving success. The experts concur that the following eight guidelines constitute fundamental steps in obtaining success in all spheres of life.

A STRONG DESIRE TO ACHIEVE HAPPINESS

We must understand that happiness comes from within and therefore has to do with our spiritual life. This in turn is reflected in other areas of life: physical, family, ministry, business, financial, et cetera. This happiness is the result of letting the Holy Spirit take control of our lives. The Lord Jesus said, *"'He who believes in me, as the scripture has said, out of his heart will flow rivers of living water.' But this He spoke concerning the Spirit, whom those believing in Him would receive; for the Holy Spirit was not yet given, because Jesus was not yet glorified"* (John 7:38-39). There is only one source of genuine happiness and that source comes from God. When an individual invites Jesus to be Lord of His life, he has continual access to that source. When some one tries to achieve happiness without God he will only achieve pleasure. That is like a glass of water in comparison to the everlasting spring of living water found in happiness. *"Jesus answered and said to her, 'If you knew the gift of God, and who it is who says to you, give me a drink, you would have asked Him, and He would have given you living water'"* (John 4:10). Only the Lord can provide each one of His children the living water of happiness. For the apostle Paul, to have a meaningful life, meant knowing Jesus Christ in a personal way, *"Yet indeed I also count all things loss for the excellence of the knowledge of Christ Jesus my Lord, for whom I have suffered the loss of all things, and count them as rubbish, that I may gain Christ"* (Philippians 3:8).

He tasted the most extra ordinary success that the world at that time could provide. However, after coming to know Jesus everything else lost its pleasure because he couldn't conceive of happiness outside of Christ.

GOOD HEALTH

"Or do you not know that your body is the temple of the Holy Spirit who is in you, whom you have from God, and you are not your own?" (1 Corinthians 6:19)

Generally, we overdo when it comes to caring for, decorating, and beautifying our homes in order to create a better environment to live. But better care must be made were God's Spirit makes His dwelling. One of the greatest enemies of one's health is stress, which is blamed for a great number of ailments and premature deaths. Other enemies of health are bad eating habits. One afternoon I was having lunch at a restaurant with a friend, Doctor Derek Prince. I asked him why he took so much care in what he ate and he told me, *"A few years ago, while I was at a fancy restaurant, I saw myself walking towards an abyss and God urged me that if I kept eating the way that I was, I would be shortening my days as many other preachers who have destroyed their bodies in these places"*. Since the, I proposed to dedicate more time to studying about my health and this has helped me to prolong my life.

God's Spirit wants to flow powerfully through a body that doesn't have internal obstacles, and we should not accept anything that would be harmful to our body's normal function. We represent God on earth, and since the world cannot see God they see Him through us. Therefore our bodies testify about us to the world. The other thing that attacks our health is denying our body the rest it requires. The Lord taught that we should dedicate six days of the week to work and one day to rest. If God Himself needed rest, how much more shall we need rest? Don't think that if you run faster you will go farther. If we follow God's pre-established principles, we can enjoy good health.

THE IMPORTANCE OF ACQUIRING GENUINE MENTAL PEACE

Mental peace is the result of a tranquil conscience. After the apostle Paul's dramatic conversion, and when presenting his defense before the priests and council of Jerusalem he said the, *"Men and brethren, I have lived in all good conscience before God until this day."* (Acts 23:1).

This testimony so perturbed the high priest Ananias that he ordered Paul's mouth to be struck, as if to show that no one can have the luxury of a tranquil conscience. Prior to his conversion, Paul was driven by religious jealousy to persecute Christians and force many of them to blaspheme the name of the Lord. He chained and incarcerated christens and even approved the death of Steven, Christianity's first martyr.

It was clear to Paul that all his past mistakes had been cancelled at the cross of Calvary. That is why he said, " *I have been crucified with Christ; it is no longer I who live, but Christ lives in me...*"Galatians 2:20

When we understand that our debt was canceled up on Calvary we discharge all feeling of guilt because we know that, *"There is therefore now no condemnation to those who are in Christ Jesus, who do not walk according to the flesh, but according to the Spirit"* (Romans 8:1). Genuine mental peace can only be experienced when you have left your burdens, at the foot of the cross.

PERSONAL SAFETY

Many are deeply concerned for their personal safety. In recent years insurance companies have grown and prospered. A prime example of man's uneasiness about his personal safety is that the doors and windows to his house have locks to preserve his possessions from any danger of theft. Furthermore, we pay taxes for the army and local police to provide for our safety. All of this adds up to the fact that many feel that their safety is threatened and ask, *"God what is happening?"* But the Psalmist declares, "... unless the Lord guards the city, the watchman stays awake in vain" (Psalm 127:1b).

When we make Jesus the Lord of our lives, He cares for and protects our families, homes, cities and nations.

A member of our church, born in Venezuela, told me

about an experience that he went through during a time in his country experienced a natural disaster in December of 1999. He said, *"Pastor, today my spirit is more joyful and thankful then ever in the Lord. When I heard the news of what was happening in Venezuela I was troubled to know that my parents were in the same area where the tragedy was occurring. So I asked the Lord to guide me in prayer and He instructed me to plead the blood of Jesus over their home and to declare a hedge of protection against any harm that could potentially destroy their home and lives. When the avalanche came it destroyed all the houses around them, and theirs was the only one left standing because it was protected and sealed by the blood of the Lamb. Nobody in the family died because they all took shelter in the house".* This brother certainly understood that the angel of the Lord encamps around those who fear Him and He defends them.

At the Lord's leading, we had a meeting with our close knit relatives and decided to anoint them by faith declaring the blood of Jesus and His protection over all of them. You too can use the authority God gave you to apply the blood of the Lamb to your whole family, and surely your home will be protected.

A BALANCED FAMILY LIFE

"Wisdom has built her house, she has hewn out her seven pillars." (Proverbs 9:1)

Marriage is as powerful as a walled city where everyone living can be safe. The leader must understand that his first priority must be his family, because when God established the marriage covenant, He delegated very specific functions to him and his spouse. The Lord entrusted the man with leadership of the family. This must not be confused with dictatorship. The man must answer as the leader for all then needs of his household. What is it worth to a man if he achieves success in his business and ministry and allows his home to disintegrate? The blessing of marriage is reflected in the Spiritual, physical and material realms of life. When we decided to get married, my wife and I determined to establish our home on the handbook of principles and guidelines necessary to maintain and sustain our family, the Word of God.

The other part of family balance is the relationship and time shared with our sons and daughters. Our children are an extension of our own character. It is necessary to spend time with them because each one must know that they can count on us for their protection and care. The Lord has given them to us to care for and develop. Many leaders of flourishing ministries have neglected their families; and their children can't count on them because church activities absorb all their time.

My wife and I have tried not to make this mistake because we understand our responsibilities and know that the success of a leader or a pastor is reflected in the testimony of his family life. Grateful children who are products of attention and care from their parents will be pillars for sustaining and enhancing the ministry that God has entrusted to the parents.

Our four daughters, Johanna, Lorena, Manuela and Sara are a great family blessing. They are all committed to the development of the vision God gave us. They know that the ministry is a family vision and each one has seriously assumed their responsibility in it.

INTEGRAL PROSPERITY

"Beloved, I pray that you may prosper in all things and be in health, just as your soul prospers" (3 John 2).

God's blessings are integral because they cover all areas of our lives, which are financial, physical, spiritual, and material. Ephesians 1:3, declares that God has blessed us with every spiritual blessing in heavenly places in Christ.

"This book of the law shall not depart from your mouth, but you shall meditate in it day and night, that you may observe to do according to all that is written in it. For then you will make your way prosperous, and then you will have good success". (Joshua 1:8)

Nobel Laureate and diplomat, Gabriela Mistral, was noted as saying, *"The Bible is the Book. I don't know how someone can live without it. We all need the Bible".* If we continually read it and believe what it says, the Bible will give us guidelines to reach God's predetermined purposes and prosperity.

In 1923, nine of the most powerful men on earth met in Chicago. Anyone could feel envious of these men since that small group of men represented seventy percent of America's wealth. They were: Charles Schwab, President of the largest steel producing company of the world; Samuel Insull, president of the largest electricity producing company; Howard Hopson, president of the largest natural gas producing company; Arthur Curten, the largest seller of wheat in the United States; Richard Whitney, president of the Stock Exchange of New York; Albert Fall, Secretary of the Interior in President Harding's Administration; Jesse

Livermore, great Wallstreet investor; Ivar Kreuger, Head of the largest monopoly of the world; and Leon Fraser, president of the International Settlements bank.

But these men, who lacked moral values and placed all their trust in uncertain riches where suddenly facing a sad reality the hopes of many rich to come to an end.

In 1948, twenty-five years after that famous meeting, Charles Schwab filed for bankruptcy and spent the last five years of his life surviving on borrowed money; Samuel Insull died in a foreign land, a fugitive of justice and penniless; Howard Hopson died an insane man; Arthur Curtin lost his economic solvency and died abroad; Richard Whitney had just been released from Sing Sing Prison; Albert Fall had just received a presidential pardon so that the could die in the company of his family and not in prison; finally Jesse Livermore and Ivar Kreuger had taken there lives just as Leon Fraser did.

What a great lesson history left us. These men all met together in the same year to be praised by the whole world, and some twenty-five years later all nine of them passed away to eternity with more sorrow than glory and all because they placed their trust in uncertain riches. The Lord Jesus Christ said, *"Assuredly, I say to you that it is hard for a rich man to enter the kingdom of heaven. And again I say to you, it is easy for a camel to go through the eye of a needle then for a rich man to enter the kingdom of God"* (Matthew 19:23-24).

When we place all that we have into God's service, He rewards us with prosperity. "Honor the Lord with your possessions, and with the first-fruits of all your increase; so your barns will be filled with plenty, and your vats will overflow with new wine" (Proverbs 3:9-10). The Lord also said that man would vainly win all the gold in the world and loose his soul. Man accomplishes nothing by acquiring money if he cannot buy salvation with it. Salvation is worth a high price that not even the most powerful of all mortal could buy. But Jesus Christ bought our salvation on Calvary. We pay absolutely nothing for it. The only condition man must meet in order to be saved is to believe in Jesus, deposit all trust in Him and to give Him his life.

Man obtains prosperity when he decides to turn with all of his heart to God, realizing that, *"For where your treasure is, there your heart will be also"* (Matthew 6:21). If our riches are established in Jesus Christ then our heart will be safe. God demands that we make a covenant with Him and that all of our life be surrendered to His service.

SELECTING OUR FRIENDS

Daniel had three friends, and when the king threatened to cut off his head, he went to them and asked them to pray. His friends backed him in prayer, and that same night God revealed to Daniel in a dream what he needed to know. It's clear that friends constitute a big support in critical moments. Proverbs 18:24 says, *"...But there is a friend that sticks closer then a brother"*.

Your friends must be fearful of God and separated from evil. If you have wicked friends it would be just as if you took an ox and a donkey and made them plow together. They would make an uneven yoke since one would pull to one side while the other would pull in the opposite direction.

In the same way, the believer may talk about God's issues while the wicked would talk about worldly issues.

The cross of Calvary tells us about relationships. Jesus

was crucified to teach us how our relationships should be. A relationship fulfills a double purpose. Calvary's cross (the timber) is made up of two logs, one vertical and one horizontal. The vertical one tells us of our relationship with God, and the horizontal one tells us of our relationship with our neighbor. A genuine relationship with God will lead us to keep a healthy relationship with our friends.

HOPE

"But for him who is joined to all the living there is hope..." (Ecclesiastes 9:4)

One of the most distorted devises of the enemy is to cause man to completely lose hope in an individual, his family, his job, or even in his country. When man loses all hope he doesn't set goals and therefore doesn't have objectives. One of the most typical examples of lost hope is found in those seeking employment, knocking on the doors of companies, only to be rejected and told they don't qualify. But the greatest motivation for all of us is that God has given us the hope to conquer our dreams while we are alive, just as the writer of Ecclesiastes declared in the above scripture. Even if a man closes the door on you, God doesn't. Above all, you must be ready to trust in Him because who ever comes to Him, He doesn't cast out. If doors on earth have been closed, they remain open in the heavenlies

Many loose hope because of a failing marriage, financial misfortune, or some other situation that reached the stage beyond their control. But there is always hope in Him, *"For a righteous man may fall seven times and rise again..."* (Proverbs 24:16). Do not accept arguments of failure that the enemy uses against you, your family, or nation.

In our case, we motivate people to recover their hope regarding our nation of Columbia, in ways that allow us to see beyond the panorama shown in the newscast. We do not repeat the negative language they use. Furthermore, we declare that Colombia is not a land of violence but of peace and blessing.

You can aspire to great conquests by applying each one of these steps in your life. Those around you will acknowledge you as a person of success because they will see that you have achieved happiness, and enjoy good health, live with genuine mental peace, possess true personal safety, have a balanced family life, have good friends, experience complete prosperity, and possess hope.

If you haven't taken any of these steps, begin now committing yourself to God and He will help you achieve success.

PART II

THE TWELVE: SYNONYMOUS WITH SUCCESS

Chapter One

THE LEADER IS THE KEY

"A true leader is one who is not afraid of change; he continually changes because to lead requires innovation." C.C.D.

THE SIGHT PLACED ON EACH PERSON

It's been proven that the model of the Twelve has given the greatest results since Jesus developed it in His earthly ministry, and this remains true in our time. The leader is the key. This was the lesson the Lord gave us by His example. Through His ministerial life He believed in people, not for what they were, but for potential that He knew existed in them. This potential came from God's Divine breath, but it was masked by different kinds of weaknesses, shortcomings or circumstances in which they found themselves.

Though Jesus could have poured His life into multitudes, He chose instead to work in the formation of the character of only twelve disciples. Like a potter with clay, for three years, He shaped each one of their characters, somewhat as Job expressed, *"Your hands created and shaped me"*. Before ascending to heaven, the Lord assembled His disciples and observed that something was still needful: Divine breath, so that they would be equipped to do evangelistic work in the different nations of the earth. That's why He told them, *"'Peace to you! As the Father has sent Me, I also send you.' And when he had said this, He breathed on them, and said to them, 'Receive the Holy Spirit'"* (John20: 21-22).

How did Jesus transform His Twelve who were apparently without refinement, education, riches or social status, to become the pillars of Christianity? The answer is simple; they were willing to be molded by Him.

As the apostle Paul explains, *"But indeed, O man, who are you to reply against God? Will the thing formed say to him who formed it, 'Why have you made me like this?' Does not the potter have power over the clay, from the same lump to make one vessel for honor and another for dishonor?"* (Romans 9:20-21).

We don't know how long it took God to form Adam's physical body, but we do know that it took the Lord Jesus three-and-a-half years to form His Twelve. He had to dig deep into their lives, just as any builder must do according to the kind of structure he is going to build. Just as an architect gives a scale model to the builder to follow his plans, Jesus left His disciples with the model of His own life to follow. Paul understood this when he said, *"Till we all come to the unity of the faith and of the knowledge of the Son of God, to a perfect man, to the measure of the stature of the fullness of Christ"* (Ephesians 4:13).

Jesus was not concerned that His disciples give admiration to Him, what He wanted most was that they emulate Him. When the apostles were in daily contact with Jesus, they were able to see in Him the ideal example they were to follow. Though all were aware that they could not surpass the Son of God it was still necessary for them to live according to a higher standard than the world. Paul said, *"Imitate me, just as I also imitate Christ"* (I Corinthians 11:1).

Jesus defined the difference between a faithful leader and a religious leader. A faithful leader is an example worth imitating. A religious leader only cares about external appearance and always justifies his actions, "Don't look at me, because as man I can fail, look to the Lord". The apostles belonged to the first group and the Pharisees belonged to the second. To which group do you belong? The vision that Jesus established goes beyond simple religiosity it is the character of Christ reproduced in us so that we may reproduce it in others.

CONSTRUCTING A BUILDING WITH HUMAN STONES

"And I also say to you that you are Peter, and on this rock I will build My church, and the gates of Hades shall not prevail against it."
(Matthew 16:18)

To build, one must first dig a foundation. The church and its foundation the Lord refers to, is not one constructed with bricks and mortar and decorated with beautiful tapestries. It is one formed by people of all cultures, races and social classes, that when they believe on Him, become members of His body. The Lord calls them, "My church" because they form part of Himself.

People are the church, and our main task is winning them to Him and carefully working with them, just as the Lord did with His disciples.

When Jesus asked, *"Who do men say that I the Son of man am?"* His disciples replied, *"Some say John the Baptist, some Elijah, and others Jeremiah or one of the prophets."* When he further asked, *"But who do you say that I am?"* Simon Peter answered, *"You are the Christ, Son of the living God."* Although Peter was the most impulsive of the Twelve, he had clear revelation about the Lord and understood that He was the promised Messiah. That's why Jesus said to him, *"Blessed are you, Simon Bar-Jonah, for flesh and blood has not revealed this to you, but my Father who is in heaven. And I also say to you, that you are Peter, and on this rock I will build my church..." (Matthew 16:17-18).* The name Simon means, "Stem, " or "reed," suggesting something unstable and changeable. Simon's main trait before becoming Peter was his impulsive character. Although his name changed, he still had the same trait. The Lord discipled him. Although in the natural he was perceived as having an unstable personality with many weaknesses and flaws, the Lord saw him as a potential, stable leader. That's why Jesus told him, "You are the rock," i.e., someone whom Jesus saw with firm character. Years later, Peter, inspired by the words Jesus, had spoken of him earlier, said to believers, *"You also, as living stones, and being built up a spiritual house, a holy priesthood..."* (1 Peter 2:5).

Peter understood he was one more rock within the building. When Jesus said, "I will build My church," He didn't mean around Jerusalem quoting prices on synagogues to find which one would be best suited for His ministry. Jesus was referring to building people. He knew the Church was not to be formed with walls but by human beings in whom Christ's character must be poured.

Jesus' church didn't have to meet; it was His custom to stop atop a mountain and preach to thousands gathered to hear His message. During more intimate encounters with his disciples He would minister to them, deep truths that remained engraved in their hearts. He built His church through a relational process, and said, *"Foxes have holes and birds of the air have nests, but the Son of man has nowhere to lay His head"* (Matthew 8:20).

EVERY PERSON IS A LEADER

The key goal to success is for each person around us to become a leader with the ability to lead others. Jesus selected twelve and didn't choose them out of sympathy, but saw in them great leadership potential. All kinds of people come to our church and some possess natural leadership skills but lack good character. Indeed, others have been injured by some of life's disappointments and have suffered tremendous setbacks, but in the hands of the Lord all often have been transformed into successful leaders.

Jesus' experience also serves as a point of reference to show us how we should form and equip our Twelve. Lets remember that when the Lord chose His Twelve, they were not the most intellectual or educated, nor of the best social standing, thus their characters and temperaments had to be developed. When Jesus selected his twelve disciples, He looked among the poor, uneducated, and illiterate, and patiently worked with them. These men selected by Jesus were violent men like James and John, called "sons of thunder" others were skeptics like Thomas, or emotional like Peter, and even traitorous like Judas. Their lives required deep work until the Lord could transform them into Christ-like examples of men.

Although Jesus ministered to the multitudes, He concentrated on the Twelve, working to make them the team who would support Him in the development of His ministry. They would be responsible for reproducing and continuing His vision. That's why as soon as Jesus reached His appointed time the Twelve dedicated themselves to the Great Commission of spreading the gospel throughout the world.

THE SECRET IS IN THE TWELVE

"The secret things belong to the Lord our God, but those things which are revealed belong to us and to our children forever, that we may do all the words of this law". (Deuteronomy 29:29)

The model of the Twelve has always been in the heart of God, and its number symbolizes government. Each number has its respective meaning. For example THREE symbolizes the Trinity, FOUR symbolizes the earthly, SEVEN symbolizes perfection, et cetera. In the same way, number TWELVE symbolizes government specifically, God's government.

Since the time of creation, God established 12 months to govern each year. Days are also governed by two periods of 12 hours each. To govern the people of Israel, God established 12 tribes. King Solomon established 12 governors, since each was obligated to provide for him and his family during each month of the year (1King 4:7). In Elijah's time, when the people surrendered to idolatry and apostasy, the prophet in his spiritual jealousy, defied the prophets of Baal to demonstrate the lack of power of their idols before the people. The true God answered with fire and accepted the sacrifice for the holocaust, to which the prophet answered by commencing the reconstruction of Jehovah's alter which lay in ruins. *"And Elijah took twelve stones, according to the number of tribes of the sons of Jacob…Then with the stones he built an alter in the name of the Lord…"* (1 Kings 18: 31-32). After preparing the holocaust, he proceeded to offer it to God in sacrifice. God quickly responded to the prophet, and through this act came the reconciliation of the people to God.

It is not by chance that the last word of the last book of the Old Testament express the manifestation of Elijah's ministry; *"Behold, I will send you Elijah the prophet before the coming of the great and a dreadful day of the Lord. And he will turn the hearts of the fathers to the children, and the hearts of the children to their fathers, lest I come and strike the earth with a curse"* (Malachi 4:5-6). I am certain that we are living in the final days when the Lord will unleash Elijah's anointing. It will fall like a shroud over the earth, and move Christian leaders in different places of the world to act with the same spirit as the prophet, having the mandate of restoring the alter of the Lord which is in ruins. If you carefully study these words, you will notice that God's alter lies in ruins in most of the nations of the world. His alter became a waste place in their hearts because of a poor testimony left by religious leaders.

For this unfortunate reason many have distanced themselves from God, having felt deceived in their faith. Today, men and women with God's zeal and mandate are committed to working, not on the walls or structure of some building, but on the people for whom Christ shed His blood.

Amid all that adversity, God is awakening the hearts of many spiritual leaders around the world with the desire to restore His alter. Men and women, who are willing to pay the price that this leadership demands, and in individual acts of faith, will choose the 12 rocks with which God will restore His ruined alter.

THE BEGINNING OF THE VISION

From the moment that the Lord released this innovative vision, my wife and I have tried to develop methods and goals that in one way or another contribute to seeing our vision realized. The only thing that has yielded results and has given us satisfaction is the plan that has come directly from God.

When the great English scientist, Sir Isaac Newton sat under a tree, a fruit fell to the ground next to him. This made him wonder why the fruit fell downward and not upwards or sideways. The thought drove him to an investigation that culminated in the discovery of the "Law of Gravity". Something similar happened to me in 1991, when the Lord took the veil of limitation off my mind and allowed me to understand the meaning of the principle of Twelve. I pondered, "Why did the Lord train twelve and not eleven or thirteen? Wasn't it better to teach a large group at the same time? The larger the number of people the faster the work could be finished. Why did He invest his time in only twelve? What secret is there in twelve?" God used all these questions to bring clarity to my life concerning the model of the Twelve. I could hear deep in my heart the voice of the Holy Spirit, "If you train twelve people and reproduce Christ's character in them which is in you, and if each one of them does the same with another twelve, and if these in turn do the same with another twelve, transmitting the same to each, you and your church will experience unprecedented growth." I immediately realized the multiplication of ministerial development that we would soon have. After God showed me a vision of multiplication at an exceptional rate, and how to do it in only one year, the only thing I could say was, "My God, this is extraordinary!'

I would have never dreamed of this phenomenal growth and its potential without the existence of this model. In order to establish a definition of this principle, it is important to note that the Lord Jesus' ministry that He had on earth inspires the model of the Twelve itself.

Chapter Two

IT'S SUPERNATURAL

"All that you desire in the natural realm, conquer it in the spiritual realm through faith and you will be astonished at what you can achieve." C.C.D.

IT'S JUST A MATTER OF BELIEVING AND OBEYING GOD

The Twelve whom the Lord discipled, learned to walk in the supernatural. It was because Christ's character was reproduced in them in all areas of their lives. For this reason the religious leaders who opposed the development of Christianity were astonished with Peter and John's boldness. They knew they were illiterate but recognized that they had been with Jesus. The model of the Twelve is the supernatural method that the Lord Jesus implemented so that His ministry would continually flow as it proceeded directly from the Father to His heart. In the precise moment that I was searching for the best strategy to win great multitudes, Jesus' experience dropped into my heart.

Before describing the way God revealed the potential of this model to me, it is important to point out in greater detail the way Jesus worked with His disciples. They went about preaching and doing miracles, within the model or government of twelve, a clear indication that supernatural power had been developed and flowed through them.

ANOINTING FOR MIRACLES

" And when He had called his twelve disciples to Him, He gave them power over unclean spirits, to cast them out, and to heal all kinds of sickness and all kinds of disease." (Matthew 10:1)

While Jesus was on earth, He asked the leper, *"What do you want me to do for you?"* The leper answered, *"Lord, if you want, you can cleanse me."* Show compassion Jesus performed the miracle. It happened in the same way to blind Bartimaeus and with many others who, guided by faith, approached Him with expectation. The Lord healed, raised the dead, cast out demons, and performed hundreds of extraordinary miracles while He was with the people. To Jesus, the people were the church.

One of the first things I learned from Jesus' experience was that when a pastor develops his ministry demonstrating these types of miracles, the news would spread throughout the community. People who are in need of a miracle will run, to hear the gospel message, and the model of Twelve will naturally allow the multitudes to be directed to the Lord's feet.

People followed Jesus for the miracles He performed. If we want to have a church with multitudes we must walk in the supernatural realm by working miracles with the power of the Holy Spirit. When the leper got close to Jesus, didn't complain about the curses that bound him. Jesus simply saw his need, acknowledged his faith and gave him what he needed. The church is supposed to have an answer for people's needs. We have proven the best way to help people, is by giving them a solution to their problems, since their faith is strengthened when they see God supply an answer to their needs.

Any father, whose son is facing an incurable disease, will repent of all his arguments and be prepared to believe in whatever will provide the miracle for his son.

On a particular Sunday, while we were celebrating our New Year's Eve service, I asked the congregation, *"How many of you are present here today because God performed a miracle for you?'* Ninety-five percent of the people raised their hands. Listening to their testimonies later, I understood that one of the best ways to spread the gospel and allow God's kingdom to be established in our community is to move in the supernatural.

A person who has received a touch from God in his body will not want to break away from the path of faith because he feels indebted to the Lord.

A MODEL OF COMPASSION

"Then Jesus went about all cities and villages, teaching in their synagogues, preaching the gospel of the kingdom, and healing every sickness and every disease among the people. But when He saw the multitudes, he was moved with compassion for them, because they were weary and scattered, like sheep having no shepherd. Then He said to his disciples, *'The harvest truly is plentiful, but the laborers are few. Therefore pray the Lord of he harvest to send out laborers into His harvest.'"* (Matthew 9:35-38)

Jesus called His twelve disciples and gave them authority to cast out demons and heal the sick. The model of Twelve was born when the Lord felt compassion for the people, because he saw them as scattered sheep without a shepherd. The church grows through evangelistic work, but the preservation of each person is received through the model of Twelve, because each leader of twelve has the ability to shepherd another twelve. If we feel compassion for the people we will be ready to care for them and pray for their needs by laying hold of the miracle they need for their lives, just as Jesus did with his disciples. With the traditional model of church, it is difficult for every member of the congregation to have access to the pastor. But through the model of Twelve everybody has contact with the pastor through his or her leader. All leaders have the same vision and ideals as the senior pastor; and everyone feels shepherded. When I understood the importance of the same compassion for the people which Jesus had, I saw the need to implement a strategy to help care for each person amid the growth that started in the church. This was how God prepared me to reveal the model of the Twelve.

PASTORING TWELVE AT A TIME

"And when He had called his twelve disciples to Him, He gave them power over unclean spirits, to cast them out, and to heal all kinds of sickness and all kinds of disease." (Matthew 10:1)

Based on Jesus' experience, the principle of the Twelve is:

A revolutionary leadership model that consists of choosing twelve men by the leader of the ministry to reproduce his character and authority in them for the development of the church's vision, thus facilitating multiplication. These twelve will select another twelve, whereupon they impart the same principles the leader has put in their lives.

Guided by Jesus' experience, who poured Himself into each disciple, we too have been developing out ministry in like manner. A good indicator that confirms our method is that the disciple reflects his teacher's character. When this disciple imparts what he has learned and experienced in his life, the other life reflects his character too. This is possible because the principle of the twelve transmits strategies, knowledge and authority, allowing the vision to be achieved in a joint way and in unity. Additionally, Jesus was exercising a direct pastorate over His Twelve. He discipled and qualified them so that they would carry out the entrusted mission according to the Lord's expectations. This pastorate is the same function we perform by applying it to each person involved in our church's teams of twelve, which number in the thousands. As a result there is direct pastoral guidance, greater care and personalized attention. Consequently, this forms the basis for all who come to the church as new believers. They commit to the same vision and feel the need and desire to become useful leaders for God's work. They are a multiplying agent in our church, which, by the way, was not possible in the traditional system.

Why are we sure that all who aspire to this kind of victorious leadership can achieve this goal? It is because in small groups it is easier to detect weakness and strengths in each individual. We minister to them to a point where they can become self-sufficient for the demands of leadership. As we train each one of our Twelve, we observe that just as God had to dig deeply in our lives to develop us as the leaders that we are today, we too have the opportunity to do the same. While working in the life of each individual, we are defining the profile of another leader.

This will be a key element that must be communicated in order for him to reproduce himself in others. If we had to work with a whole congregation simultaneously, the job would be both impossible and expensive, forcing us to quit before reaching our desired results. When this important labor is done in groups of twelve, results are optimal in terms of quality and quantity since multiplication is faster and we have more time to observe growth.

If you desire a small ministry, God will act according to that design. But if you want God to entrust you with a large ministry with unlimited outreach, you must understand that the Lord will dig deeply into your life, and use you to do the same to those who are going to be your support team.

Since we implemented the principle of Twelve, our church has experienced the greatest growth known in Colombia's Christian history. The vision of cells has been developing at a phenomenal growth rate. From the small number of 70 home groups we have surpassed 15,000 cells statistically confirmed in the city of Bogotá alone.

This growth has not happened because the doors of homes have spontaneously opened to us. It is because the model of twelve has facilitated to the preparation of strong leaders who have been willing to take on His commitment by using the doors of opportunity that are open to them.

Growth is also due to the fact that in this model everyone is challenged in his or her personal and ministerial objective. There isn't a single person involved in a group of Twelve who doesn't want to grow. Furthermore, when someone sees others growing, he feels motivated to achieve his own multiplication goals so as not to be left behind.

When someone discovers the power and the authority that can be developed by being a leader of twelve persons, he then desires to enable others to acquire their own group of twelve.

We may further define this model as the principle that drives the growth dynamics for the contemporary church. In my own experience, I believe that the model of Twelve is the strategy that will sustain with the cell vision as the development of Christ's church in the twenty-first century.

Chapter Three

THE CONQUEST OF NATIONS

"The principle of Twelve is a concept from God imprinted in Scripture as an inspiration for proper government, and a strategy for the conquest of nations." C.C.D.

AN EMINENTLY BIBLICAL STRATEGY

The principle of Twelve not only comes from God at a specific historic time, for leaders willing to embrace it, but it is also printed in Scripture as an enduring inspiration.

PRINCIPLE OF GOVERNMENT

"Moreover He said, 'I am the God of your father the God of Abraham, the God Isaac, and the God of Jacob.' And Moses hid his face, for he was afraid to look upon God." (Exodus 3:6)

God revealed himself to Moses as the God of Abraham, Isaac, and Jacob. Abraham represents the man of faith, Isaac the man of sacrifice, and Jacob represents the man of government. Notice that God made Abraham the following promise: *"No longer shall your name be called Abram, but your name shall be Abraham; for I have made you a father of many nations...but God said to Abraham, 'Do not let it be displeasing in your sight because of the lad or because of your bond woman. Whatever Sarah has said to you, listen to her voice; for in Isaac your seed shall be called'"* (Genesis 17:5; 21:12). But it was necessary for Isaac to have Jacob. From Jacob twelve sons would be born, who would later become the patriarchs for the fulfillment of the promise. Each son of Jacob constituted one of the twelve tribes of Israel.

Inspired by this government principle, Moses guided the people of Israel to the Exodus journey from Egypt. Arriving at the border of Canaan, Moses selected twelve spies to inspect the land they were about to enter. And when they returned, they reported everything they observed in Canaan; it's terrain, the characteristics of the people who inhabited the land, whether they were strong or weak, whether the inhabited cities were encampments or fortified places, and so on. With this team representing the symbol of government, the Lord gives us strategies to conquer any city or nation. As with Moses, the model of twelve provides a strategic plan with a conquest of ministry in our city, nation, or the rest of the world.

The government principle reflected in the model Twelve helps us develop a spiritual cartography, identifying which demonic powers work in which regions. We cannot arrive at a place and arrogantly build a church saying, "Because we come in the name of our denomination, God will prosper the work of our hands." Undoubtedly, God works and performs great exploits on our behalf, but there is one prior condition to fulfill, which we cannot overlook: discover how and with which spiritual allies the adversary has been working in the target region.

The Lord told the people of Israel, through Joshua, *"Every place that the sole of your foot will tread upon, I have given you, as I said to Moses"* (Joshua 1:3).

In other words, God was telling them to "*conquer.*"

But the people had to know who were the inhabitants of the land, and they had to measure their strength to develop proper strategies to defeat them. Only then could they set up their tents on conquered places further analyzing the principle of government within the model of Twelve, and gleaning from Moses' experience, we observe that the leader chosen by God commissions his Twelve along the following:

MAKE A GENERAL DIAGNOSIS

One must thoroughly observe the land, analyze it, and understand the condition of the people living there. This process helps to identify their spiritual bondages, i.e., whether they are slaves to idolatry, practice sorcery, witchcraft or any other vice, and are skeptical of the things of God. It is imperative to know this framework before you prepare to evangelize.

KNOW THE CONDITION OF THE PEOPLE

Are the people strong or weak? What gives them strength? In which philosophies are they raised, are they atheists, communists or spiritually opposed to God.

Lets remember that these are factors, which harden the hearts of people and make them resist into the gospel. At this point it may be easy to penetrate them with the gospel if they have lost trust in past structures, such as money, rites or other traditions. For example, in our country our people began to look for new spiritual alternatives. One woman said, "I threw away all the candles that I lit up to the Virgin Mary because she didn't answer my prayers." In these cases, aggressive evangelism is the key to conquest, and the Twelve can develop it with authority.

DETERMINE THE SCOPE OF THE CONQUEST

Are the people few or many? Some say, "Quantity doesn't matter, only the quality." Moses cared whether the people he challenged were few or many, because he knew that he had been called to conquer nations.

The model of the Twelve allows us to have great objectives and reaffirms that evangelism must be carried out first in great urban cities and from there into smaller towns, but we must think big.

DISCERN THE ENVIRONMENT OF THE TERRITORY

Is it a land of blessings or curses, i.e., is the land good or bad? We must know which curses exist in the region and how to cut them off.

Solomon said that a curse is never caused without a reason. One of the reasons God promised Moses He would deliver the land of Canaan to the people of Israel was because Canaan had completely removed itself from Him. The people had surrendered to worshiping every kind of idol and performed diabolical practices such as passing offspring through fire, and offering them to Baal. They had contaminated the land in such a way that God's wrath was turned against them. Moses and the people of Israel had to cleanse the land of all its spiritual contamination.

This is an example of the struggle we must fight today against evil spiritual forces. Paul said, *"For we do not wrestle against flesh and blood, but against principalities, against powers, against the rulers of darkness of this age, against hosts of wickedness in the heavenly places"* (Ephesians 6:12).

DO AN ANALYSIS THROUGHOUT THE CITY

What is the status of the city? There is a difference between a city and a nation. We can talk about a curse on a city on the one hand, and a curse on a whole nation on the other. Demonic powers act territorially. The Israelites knew that walled cities like Jericho were strongholds against God, and when Jericho was conquered, they began to see it as a cursed city. Therefore, all that comprised the city had to be destroyed. Given the cursed condition of this city, when Joshua conquered it with Israel. He declared, *"Cursed be the man before the Lord who rises up and builds this city Jericho; he shall lay its foundation with his firstborn, and with his youngest he shall set up its gates"* (Joshua 6:26). Later, the curse relapsed on Hiel the Bethelite, when he decided to rebuild Jericho.

KNOW IF THE TERRAIN IS FERTILIZED FOR REVIVAL

What is the status of the terrain? Here I make a reference to the land itself. Questions that should be asked are: Is the land ready for spiritual harvest? Can we find fruit in the people or not? Armed with the answers to these questions, are we ready to conquer the nation with the model of Twelve?

Moses ordered the spies to take fruit from the land to determine whether the land was good and its fruit abundant. As part of the report, the commissioned spies returned with a cluster of grapes so big that they had to be carried by two men. However, they also discovered the land was inhabited with giants, and this frightened them. So the report of the most of the spies was negative. Israel sinned by looking at things with the human eye, thereby abandoning God's perspective of what He could do through them. They therefore concluded it was a land that was not going to be easy to conquer.

The same type of thing occurs today when many regions of the world are declared "preacher's cemeteries." These are statements that should not come out of our lips. Many of the commissioned spies did not see through eyes of faith. Fortunately, Joshua and Caleb were different, and their faith helped Israel conquer the land.

Success is not achieved because of negative confessions and beliefs that some believers hold. These hinder the work of the mission. Scoffers may ask why you and your church are going to work with cells. They may argue that the principle of the Twelve doesn't work for you; it might make sense in Korea or Colombia, but not where you live! But just as God did with Israel, He has given us strategies to conquer nations, and the model of Twelve is the one many all over the world are implementing during this time in the history of the Church. When this godly principle gains root in our hearts, we won't allow ourselves to be discouraged by anyone.

Unfortunately, ten of the twelve spies sent by Moses weren't allowed to enter the Promised Land because they didn't have the same spirit as Joshua and Caleb. Later, Joshua selected twelve and asked each one to build an alter, to establish a memorial, to commemorate the Divine protection that aided the great conquest of the Promised Land. If you choose this vision, God will also help you conquer your city and nation.

Chapter Four

RAISING UP THE BEST LEADERS (1)

"The capacity of leadership is measured by the way the leader strategically reproduces his vision in others."
C.C.D.

THE IMPORTANCE OD GOOD SELF ESTEEM

"...I will build my church..." (Matthew 16:18)

The word, build means to shape or construct. When we were finishing the construction of the building that we have across the street from the church, I went up to the last floor and carefully observed the stacks of bricks that were going to be used to raise the walls.

The Lord showed me different piles of bricks and had me compare them with the bricks already set in the building of the church.

He then asked me, "Son, what difference do you see between this pile of bricks and those set in the wall of the church?' I answered, "Lord, the bricks in the church were strategically placed following a plan, but these ones are simply piled up." The Lord then asked, "Which ones are worth more?' I replied, "Lord, the ones already strategically in place." Then He said, "That is what I want you to do in the church. I don't want piled up believers just occupying pews, I want believers to establish their strategic place within the body of Christ."

The Lord sees believers as living stones He doesn't see us as a conglomerate, but as individually important stones in this church of Christ. When undertaking a construction project, a design by an architect is required. When we meet with an architect prior to building the church, He took our ideas and worked with them to make a blueprint. After being approved by the city planning department, scale models were made which were handed to the builder with instruction to start the work. In the same way, God considers each individual as part of His construction, having generated the master blueprint Himself. He then handed it to us as a guide from which to build. Within the blueprint, He made provision for the need to have a support system, which we refer to as the Twelve. The Twelve are raised up to build strategically, and that's why we train our Twelve who in turn train another twelve, and all are considered living stones.

"For we are His workmanship, created in Christ Jesus for good works, which God prepared beforehand that we should walk in them." (Ephesians 2:10)

Questions that may arise from those desiring this vision include: How do we know who is going to be a part of our Twelve? What do we do to get those people involved? Who will be an essential part of the ministry? Without a doubt, leadership is measured by the way we reproduce. The seal of a pastorate is reflected in the people developed in the church.

When David tried to form his first congregation, businessmen didn't come to him, nor did military strategists or intellectuals. Those who surrounded him were in debt, bitter of spirit, and full of problems. They were the people he was entrusted to Shepard. From that group arose the bravest men, those who gave their lives for him, these same types of people will come to us too; deeply needy souls with broken hearts, men and women who may tell you, "Brother, I'm finished, I want to take my life, I am tired, I am burdensome to everybody!" These will become your crucible of fire and God will test you to see if you love them because only love can transform them. Consequently, each will be a great challenge to your leadership because you will have to develop them. If you don't have the experience, you will acquire it through patience and practice.

As a leader, practice will show you how to handle and develop each person under your care. Your advantage is that you already intimately know the Lord, whereas the new recruits are just starting to open their eyes. New ones arrive with their eyes shut and rely on you to have the answer to their needs. There are various key elements to watch for in nurturing and caring for those who will be your best candidates, and will in turn form the genuine team. We will see the first five in this chapter.

VALUE THEM AS PERSONS

Your disciples must be valued for who they are, and not so much for what they can do. Generally, we err when we appreciate those around us for the fruit they produce. If they show no fruit we are not interested in them. In spite of all the weaknesses and failures of a child, the father loves his son because he is his son.

The mistake of many parents is that they center their attention on the most exceptional or compliant child and compare him against the others, "You are not like your brother. He is admirable". How do you think a child feels when he is constantly being compared with his brother?

He feels bad. I have four daughters and as a father, I love them equally. They are all important to me and I love them not for what they do, but because they are my daughters. You should behave in the same way with each disciple that God assigns you to in your group of Twelve.

Appreciate them for who they are, treat them like persons, invest time in them, give them love and affection so they don't feel that you count on them only for cell meeting reports, but that they are truly valuable elements in the organization.

BELIEVE IN THEM

Learn to believe your group of Twelve. When people first arrive they may not appear successful, most may have failure on their faces. However, we must see them with eyes of faith, visualizing what Christ can do in them. Paul says, *"Him we preach, warning every man and teaching every man in all wisdom, that we may present everyman perfect in Christ Jesus. To this end, I also labor, striving according to His working which works in me mightily"* (Colossians 1:28-29).

Paul leaned to see people through eyes of faith. He warned and taught that all wisdom is in the doctrine of God's Word. He did an intense work in each person because his goal was to present each man perfect in Jesus Christ. To achieve this purpose, Paul said, *" To this end I also labor, striving according to His working which works in me mightily"* (Colossians 1:29).

The apostle was conscious of the need to work hard in the discipling of each individual, i.e., to call on them, be patient with them, and to fight against powers of darkness that were set against them until he achieved victory. If we desire to disciple and mentor others, we must strive for their deliverance until they reach the height of Christ's fullness for their lives. Perform as Paul, whose spiritual battle was fortified by the power of Christ inside him.

RECOGNIZE THEIR TRIUMPHS

The triumphs of those around us must not only be recognized, but we should recognize that this reflects on the leaders as well. How many times has your team achieved great victories and you have never recognized their efforts? Someone told me, "When I was a child I learned good grades and presented them to my father, but he never congratulated me, he always told me, 'Remember, next time they have to be better.' When I achieved a conquest, there was never a congratulatory word, on the contrary, he said, 'Now you have to aim higher!'" According to this individual, up to this day he has never managed to satisfy his father.

As a leader, learn to recognize the achievements of those who work with you and who make up your team. Paul comments, *"Knowing, beloved brethren, your election by God. For our gospel did not come to you in word only, but also in power, and in the Holy Spirit and in much assurance, as you know what kind of men we were among you for your sake"* (1 Thessalonians 1:4-5).

Paul praised the Thessalonians because he knew them and loved them, and understood the commitment and perseverance required to establish their Christian walk. Because Jesus' gospel was received in words and power, the Thessalonians could value and appreciate the apostle's heart. This is why Paul expresses his praise to them. Furthermore, when the Lord wrote to the seven churches in the book of Revelation, He gave them the acknowledgment each one deserved, even though He also had to reprove them.

To the church of Philadelphia He says: *"I know your works. See, I have set before you an open door, and no one can shut it; for you have a little strength, have kept My word, and have not denied My name"* (Revelation 3:8).

The Lord recognized that that church was weak. Nevertheless, He praised them because they had kept His word and were not ashamed of Him, nor did they deny his name. In the same way, it is important to recognize those around you and to give them a voice of support encouraging and motivating them to keep going.

UNDERSTANDING THEM

The leader must understand each member of the team when they go through their struggles. Paul tells the Philippians,

"Let nothing be done through selfish ambition or conceit, but in lowliness of mind of mind let each esteem others better than himself." (Philippians 2:3)

When a person goes through a test we should try to put ourselves in his shoes. I have seen some leaders use harsh discipline, "Because you failed, you deserve an admonition!" They shame that person to the point of nearly alienating him. One who's treated this way can be destroyed. Learn something important before using drastic measures, think of the one who failed as if he were you, and ask yourself, "How would I like to be treated?" This is how you place yourself in someone else's shoes. If we learn to do this, we won't become impatient judges, but merciful leaders.

When someone is struggling and fighting battles, our duty as leaders should be to motivate him to come out victorious on the other side and not be defeated in battle. When a soldier is wounded in war his comrade should not give him the coup de grace, the finishing blow, but help him and take him out of the battle if necessary. Cure your wounded and they will never forget the favor. Give the deathblow, and their blood will claim vengeance over you.

WATCH OVER THE GROUP'S UNITY

One of the primary and continuous tasks of the leader must be to keep the group united.

"Endeavoring to keep the unity of the Sprit in the bond of peace. There is one body and one spirit, just as you were called in one hope of your calling; one Lord, one faith, one baptism; one God and Father of all, who is above all, and through all, and in you all." (Ephesians 4:3-6)

Paul says that we must work carefully and diligently to guard the unity of the Spirit. What breaks the unity of the Spirit? Sin does. Keeping the group united requires preserving them in holiness. At this stage of development, it then becomes necessary to bring in the Encounter (to be discussed later) and properly minister to each individual in their personal struggles so that you may identify which disputes the devil has raised against them and which ones are affecting unity.

What affected the unity of ancient Israel? Sin always did. In the first battle at Ai, when they began pursuing the enemy, they advanced as a strong army, and were unified as a single man. This is how they conquered enemy nations and faced the walled city of Jericho. However, when they continued to fight the small city of Ai, its inhabitants rose up and broke them defeating and killing many in battle.

After this defeat the Israelites inquired of the Lord, "What happened?" God responded, "All Israel has sinned". The unity had been affected by the sin of a single man, Achan. The sin of a single man can have an adverse affect on the whole group, and this was well understood by Paul when he said, "Endeavoring to keep the unity of the Spirit in the bond of peace" (Ephesians 4:3). God wants the church, its leadership and the cell group to maintain holiness. No leader must tolerate or consent to sin in any of its members.

Chapter Five

RAISING UP THE BEST LEADERS (2)

"Victory is a conquest of man himself, but a great victory is the result of teamwork." C.C.D.

Remember, the group of Twelve forms the best team in the development of the vision. Consider other guidelines to help establish a team that will take you to victory. The following are additional key elements to consider when raising up the best team.

GIVE THEM A HAND OF SUPPORT

When a leader is conscious of the fact that his work consists of discipling all aspects of an individual in his care, he will realize that looking after one's needs is fundamental to forming the best leaders. Paul said,

"Fulfill my joy, by being likeminded, having the same love, being of one accord, of one mind." (Philippians 2:2)

When someone on my team is in a low performance mode, I call him aside to talk and take note of any urgent needs or struggles he may be facing. We must understand that they want to be fruitful, but pressures may become too great for them to face alone.

Friendship ties with a team of Twelve, allows for and requires mutual transparency, so that together problems can be worked out and difficulties overcome. As a leader of

Twelve, not only am I concerned about the fruit the team can produce, but also my wife and I commit to watch over the needs of each individual.

THE PASTOR, LIKE A COACH, KNOWS THE NEEDS OF THE GROUP AND LEARNS TO INVEST IN THEM

Many Christian leaders concentrate on numbers, and only focus on the expectation of the church growth. Though numerical growth is important, it is useless to have a church full of people who complain for lack of pastoral care. You can never ignore the human condition of each individual and must understand that some may arrive with personal problems that must be addressed. Again, a group grows strong when its leader is attentive to its needs.

GIVE PRIORITY TO THE NEEDS OF THE TEAM

It is not enough to know the needs of those who compose your support team, but to show your interest by providing solutions, especially spiritual ones.

"If indeed you have heard him and have been taught by him, as the truth in Jesus: That you put off, concerning your former conduct, the old man which grows corrupt according to the deceitful lusts, and be renewed in the spirit of your mind, and that you put on the new man which was created according to God, in true righteousness and holiness." (Ephesians 4:21-24)

It should be a fundamental priority to understand the spiritual needs of the group and observe whether or not they are receiving biblical doctrine. This is reflected in a change from their past way of living. When a person's life is renewed, his past remains behind him and there is a full transformation in his mind, which he demonstrates in loving justice and truth.

CONCENTRATE ON THEM

A natural desire of each person is for their leader to watch over them, and to concentrate on their needs and personal development. As a leader, you must have your five senses set on the success of your group and work hard to achieve it. Paul says, *"My little children, for whom I labor in birth again until Christ is formed in you."* (Galatians 4:19)

Paul did not for an instant divert his attention from his disciples. It is not enough for the leader to go to the meetings, he must concentrate on fully forming each individual, and this demands an investment of time and continual prayer.

The apostle mentions that this developmental work caused labor pains. This is very intense pain, so intense that the Lord Jesus Christ compares the most difficult period of human history, the great tribulation, to labor pains. Paul said, "I am suffering labor pains because I want you born in Christ again." You are called to beget your Twelve in the gospel of Christ, to pray for them, and labor for them until Christ is formed in them.

DEVELOPING FRIENDSHIP TIES

Proverbs 18:24 says, *"A man who has friends must show himself friendly, but there is a friend who sticks closer than a brother."* The vision of the Twelve is consistent with that biblical principle. It is a vision of unity, brotherhood, and solidarity. The leader can succeed with his group when he presents himself as the person in which each one can put their trust.

"If then you count me as a partner, receive him as you would me."(Philemon 1:17)

Here, Paul addresses Philemon, essentially saying that if you count on me as your partner, a tight relationship must be maintained.

I consider the members of my group of Twelve as friends. We share things together and don't feel like strangers because friendship ties bind us together, even though I'm their spiritual leader. The vision of the Twelve facilitates cohesion among members, sharing ideas and goals that motivate us to do a coordinated job based on our genuine friendship. You know that those around you are your friends when they open their hearts to reveal secrets and internal struggles. I am sure that the members of my team have deposited their trust in me as their leader, friend, and spiritual guide, and in that secrets don't exist between us. It is similar to the relationship I have with my daughters. A great level of trust attaches me to them, so that there are no secrets among us. Amongst the team there must be a transparent relationship and that is why we must treat all of them as friends.

SUCCESS IS DETERMINED BY THE TEAM

The vision of the Twelve is an integral system in which each member plays an important role and is key element. This vision does not allow for unilateral work that's usually done in a traditional system. Success through this vision is obtained when the leader involves everyone as a whole body in achieving his goals. No one obtains victory single-handedly. Each battle won when achieving objectives, depends on the communal work between the leader and his disciples.

"If I am not an apostle to others, yet doubtless I am to you. For you are the seal of my apostleship in the Lord." (1Corinthians 9:2)

Paul's success and his seal as an apostle was how the church developed in Corinth. Paul said that his seal as an apostle was in them, and what he had to show for his ministry was in them. Likewise, you too show the seal of leadership in your group. The conduct, fruit and development of each person who forms your team constitute the seal that indicated your work as a leader.

STRONG LEADERS MAKE STRONG MINISTRIES

Our task, though it's the most noble and beneficial is not easy. It demands dedication, discipline, devotion and above all, staying firm while aiming at your objectives. *"Therefore I run thus: not with uncertainty. Thus I fight: not as one who beats the air. But I discipline my body and bring it into subjection, lest, when I have preached to others, I myself should become disqualified."* (1 Corinthians 9:26-27)

Paul saw his leadership of others as a metaphor for running a spiritual race. He saw them struggling with the same intensity, but admonished them that his objective was not for a corruptible crown, trophy, prize, but that he was competing because he longed for the day His Lord would tell him, "Well done good and faithful servant you have finished the race."

In the same way, you must be an example for others to follow. I heard it said, " The rhythm of the boss is the rhythm of the enterprise, the rhythm of the leader is the rhythm of the group, the rhythm of the pastor is the rhythm of the church." You are called to take your church and your group to a great rhythm. Don't be a lazy leader. Learn the secrets of prayer, fasting, vigils, intercession, ministration, encounters, consolidation, and all the elements integral to this mission.

As a leader you must be submerged in the vision and walk a t a good rhythm. Don't delegate everything. You must go to the front and lead all of the important aspects of the vision. If you are a strong leader, those following you will be as strong as you and this will take them to success.

Chapter Six

RAISING UP THE BEST LEADERS (2)

"The people under your leadership are like rough diamonds, your work as a leader is to polish them so that they shine." C.C.D.

FOCUSING TOWARD SUCCESSFUL GROWTH

When members of the group feel valued as individuals and priority has been given to helping them with their needs, they are ready to develop as leaders. The following factors, if applied, will determine the outcome of the team's purpose.

TEACH THEM TO GROW

The growth of each individual is possible but only with dedicated teaching efforts. In other words, growth is taught, i.e., people grow as they are guided and motivated towards a goal. As a leader, you must develop the members of your group in the same way a father teaches his sons.

There a re many stages in the process of growth. For example, first a child crawls, then he takes his first steps, then he walks, and then he runs. In each stage the father stimulates development and celebrates when the child advances to the next step, such as when the child learns to stand by himself. This helps immensely in the process of growth, and it works best when the motivation is accompanied by affection, words of encouragement and a good attitude. Likewise, your team must have continuous stimulation to grow.

Paul comments, *"Yet indeed I also count all things loss for the excellence of the knowledge of Christ Jesus my Lord, for whom I have suffered the loss of all things, And count them as rubbish, that I may gain Christ."* (Philippians 3:8)

First of all, Paul helps the Philippians to grow using himself as their example. The members of the team will be able to grow in many ways, even with self-discipline. The greatest growth impact occurs as a result of the primary leader's examples, which are demonstrated through his life and his actions. That is what we are called to do as leaders to show that all things in this world are secondary, and that we have chosen to loose all things in order to win the most important thing, the Lord Jesus Christ.

In the second instance, Paul teaches that the is making an effort to be found in Christ, not by his own justice, which is by the law, but by faith, *"...and be found in Him not having my own righteousness, which is from the law, but that which is through faith in Christ..."* (Philippians 3:9).

One of the primary guidelines the leader must instill in his disciples is that their salvation will not come through their deeds but through their faith. The group must be people of faith who act above reason and logic, because only faith produces salvation.

Third, Paul tried to instruct and encourage them in their faith to develop a personal and intimate relationship with him, "That I may know Him."

Leaders have the challenge of giving members of their group the opportunity to know the truth and that truth must be centered on the person of Jesus Christ. That's why time must be invested in the formation of each individual opening the scriptures to them and teaching them biblical truths.

That's why I write books in order to teach individuals the great truths of the word.

Fourth, Paul shows that the resurrection power was real in his life (Philippians 3:10) and his great desire was that the Philippians come to know that power. Paul teaches that the nature within us is revived through the power of Jesus. These are essential truths that must be taught by the leader to the members of this group.

Fifth, the apostle Paul points out that he had not achieved perfection, but he persevered so that he might, "…lay hold of that for which Christ Jesus has also laid hold of me" (Philippians 3:12). This was Paul's way of communicating to the Philippians that he had not yet achieved anything but had to keep striving to fulfill God's purpose on earth. Paul's attitude must be considered by the leader and taught that one must not rest, and that the goal is not exclusively for their Twelve but that they must continue pressing on until His purposes are fully established.

Sixth, Paul taught the Philippians that what had already been conquered was no longer a challenge (Philippians 3:13). The leader must make sure that his disciples fix their sights on that which is ahead. Often leaders waste time resting on past glories, and this is time which should be invested in new goals; *"Brethren, I do not count myself to have apprehended; but one thing that I do, for getting those things which are behind and reaching forward to those things which are ahead"* (Philippians 3:13). We must concern ourselves with what is left to conquer.

Seventh, *"I press toward the goal for the prize of the upward call of God in Christ Jesus"* (Philippians 3:14).

We see that Paul didn't lose sight of his goal and he motivated the Philippians to keep pressing toward the same mark. Eighth, Paul says that everyone that is perfect must act mature in all things, and if in anything one feels differently, God would reveal it to them (Philippians 3:15). One clear indicator of perfection achieved in the process of growing is the quality of unity between the group and its leader. This indeed reflects spiritual maturity.

ONE'S DEVELOPMENT
IS REFLECTED IN GROWTH

Every leader with noble and defined goals always aims toward joint development. The progress of each team member equates to the success of the whole group, and subsequently to the success of the church.

Paul tells Timothy,

"Let not one despise your youth, but be an example to the believers in the word, in conduct, in love, in spirit, in faith, in purity. Till I come. Give attendance to reading, to exhortation, to doctrine. Do not neglect the gift that is in you, which was given to you by prophesy with the laying on of hands with the eldership. Meditate on these things; give yourself entirely to them that your progress may be evident to all. Take heed to your self and to the doctrine. Continue in them for in doing this you will save both yourself and those that hear you." (1 Timothy 4:12-16)

Again, here we find Paul giving fundamental guidelines for the groups' development. First, don't let anyone despise you or consider you a charlatan, as one who says one thing and does another. Furthermore, let no one despise you because of your youth, but let them see someone who is diligently developing and growing.

Second, be a good example to other believers. The advice Paul gives Timothy is to appear before others as one to be imitated in word, conduct, love, spirit, faith and purity. The word of the believer, especially the leaders', must be a word of faith, and his behavior must prove exemplary so that no one points to him negatively. Love must be demonstrated and not simply spoken. This display of love must be shown with a drive of a renewed spirit and not guided by his flesh. One's behavior must always be associated with faith and purity, the kind Jesus demands of His disciples.

Third, be given to reading, encouragement, and teaching. These three are necessary for individual and team development. Our culture is not given to reading, however, as leaders concerned for the development of our people, we must motivate our team to do so. Let your reading goal, as minimum, be one book per week. Education, i.e. the teaching of doctrine must be from both the sacred Scriptures and all subjects that help in our spiritual edification. Generally, the education people receive is a bombardment of negative messages through radio, television, and the work place. As Christian leaders we must change this panorama by teaching the good news of salvation, the Word of God.

Fourth, Paul advises Timothy, "Don't neglect the gift that is in you." The leader must always acknowledge that the members of his team have gifts and they must be developed. Each one must nurture his gift with the leader's support. These gifts are imparted to each individual by the laying on of hands and should be an operation within this setting, following the guidelines set out in Scripture. Paul further admonishes the church in Corinth that all should desire these gifts (1 Corinthians 14:1).

Fifth, keep your life closely guarded. Man's worst enemy is not the devil or the world, but himself. The enemy cannot make you sin. He tries bringing distractions in the form of temptations that can create blind spots to that you slip and fall, but you are ultimately the one who will decide to yield to those temptations or not. It is dangerous to play with temptation. If you know that you are in a compromising situation it is important to flee from it.

Your strength is your doctrine. You must apply it by not allowing misguided arguments to dissuade you, and you must guard against self-imposed religion meant to divert you from the faith. Many false doctrines have proliferated, such as one that claims once you accept Jesus as Savior you are saved and therefore may sin and do whatever you please, without damnation. This is a foolish argument and a perversion of God's doctrine. God's doctrine must be diligently followed and in so doing a man will save himself and those around him.

FORM EXEMPLARY LEADERS

Brilliant leaders create brilliant churches. Each individual person arrives at the church in the rough. But the leader is given charge, as God's instrument, to polish the vessel until the individual becomes a precious diamond who shines on his own and is ready to polish others.

"For though I am free from all men, I have made myself a servant to all, that I might win the more."
(1 Corinthians 9:19)

One of Paul's greatest concerns was the development of brilliant and skilled leaders, and he used different strategies to accomplish this task. He communicated with them on their level in order that he might win them. Being free from all men, he became everyone's slave, thus learning the secret of serving. As a leader, you too must learn to serve. If a person does not have a servant's heart he will scarcely achieve an honorable position. One, who cannot serve, doesn't deserve to be served. Paul didn't spare any effort in demonstrating this important stage in the process of developing others in Christ. Furthermore, he became a gentile to win, Gentiles, he was also frank and open with the Jews to win them. These strategies were effective and persuaded many people to come to the feet of Jesus Christ.

GUIDE THEM TO SUCCESS

Success is not for just a few, and God in His infinite mercy planned triumph for all, regardless of race, upbringing or social status. The work of the leader must be to motivate each member of the team to be aware that success awaits him, but that he must work to achieve it. There isn't a person in the world, which in one way or another does not desire success. Many try to attain success erroneously, but with the model of Twelve, we have guidelines, so that every one aims at the perfect target. Furthermore, Paul tells the Corinthians, *"I planted the seed, Apollos watered it, but God gave the increase."* (1 Corinthians 3:6)

Team success requires guidelines to win through collaboration, and to avoid jealous competition. Paul is saying that one preaches, another is converted, but it is God who provides growth. While we are on the same team, the prize belongs to all. When a team competes and wins the trophy. It is for the whole team. In this model, personal success belongs to the entire group, so that the success of the group becomes a personal goal.

When we work in unity, the circumstances become irrelevant. Motivate the group to do the work in a spirit of unity, as would an athletic team competing for a championship.

TEACH SPIRITUAL DISCIPLINE

The greatest growth dimension of the group is measured on the spiritual level. Thus, the leader has the imperative to grow too, learning discipline that will later be taught to those he mentors. Just as a father establishes rules of conduct inside his home, when functioning in the realm of God's kingdom, God left us rules and guidelines that we must follow for our development in order to live in harmony with one another. The same love that God deposited in our lives challenges us to pursue the common welfare of others. The Lord summarized every law in two commandments: Love God with all your mind, soul and strength and love your neighbor as you love yourself. God's disciplines are not laborious, because they don't produce slavery, but they produce full freedom. *"For my yoke is easy, and my burden is light"* (Matthew 11:30).

CREATE AN ATMOSPHERE THAT
BRINGS OTHERS INTO LEADERSHIP

If we are going to encourage others to become leaders, establishing teaching guidelines isn't enough, but their learning environment must be inviting and motivation towards leadership. The atmosphere exerts a definitive influence on the achievement of this important objective. The leader and his group must use resources and strategies that will aid in their personal and ministerial development.

"And the believers were increasingly added to the Lord, multitudes of both men and women." (Acts 5:14)

When a pleasant and inviting atmosphere exists in a meeting it attracts people, and they are converted to the Lord. In our experience, the appropriate environment for this process is the homogenous group: men draw men, women draw women, youth draw youth, couples, draw couples, children draw children, and in this environment they desire to become leaders.

CHALLENGE THEM WITH A HIGH GROWTH MODEL

The vision of the Twelve doesn't allow for conformist schemes. Every leader should not be afraid to attempt the impossible and must have great goals and aspirations.

No one should conform to a low standard of leadership. The potential of each person is too immense to waste on small things.

"Also a multitude gathered from the surrounding cities to Jerusalem, bringing sick people and those who were tormented by unclean spirits and they were all healed." (Acts 5:16)

This was possible because of the measure of faith that the apostles demonstrated. They prayed for the sick and they were healed. They rebuked demonic spirits and the people were delivered. They prayed for lepers and they were cleansed. They left examples of the highest level of leadership, and the dimension of miracles is a level to which to we must aspire. Remember, it all depends upon the leader's example. If a leader performs at a level of five on a 1-to-10 scale he will not attract others who have learned to receive from a nine on the same scale. They will eventually prefer to gravitate to a leader at their level or higher. You must project confidence to be a great leader, since that's the only way a person at a high level of maturity will want to follow you. If a leader doesn't have at least five people following him, he is not working the model of leadership correctly. Only someone with followers, in this case, a solid group of 12, will exert true leadership qualities. A leader without followers is not a true leader, just as one is not a pastor if he doesn't have a church to shepherd, nor is one a president without a nation to govern. If you aspire to leadership you must have followers.

A HIGH LEVEL OF LEADERSHIP
IS CHARACTERIZED BY CONTROL
OF THE VISION

Since the beginning of this book I have talked about the importance of associating successful leadership with a defined vision. There is no leadership without a vision just as there is no vision without leadership. Although Paul began as a persecutor of the church and its believers, he eventually had the opportunity to meet Christ in a personal way. As a result, Paul was fully consumed with Christ's vision, and that's why a real part of our Christian doctrine was revealed through this great man.

"For I consider that I am not at all inferior to the most eminent apostles. Even though I am untrained in speech, yet I am not in knowledge. But we have been thoroughly manifested among you in all things." (2 Corinthians 11:5-6)

Paul didn't acquire leadership nor was his position as apostle given by good fortune. It was a compensation for his commitment and struggle. To get to the summit of the leadership mountain, requires strategic work, developing tenacity, knowledge and sacrifice. Although he was crude in speech he had great knowledge of the vision. It is not enough to just have an idea of the vision it is important and necessary to be consumed by it until it becomes a way of life for the entire team.

A HIGH LEVEL OF LEADERSHIP IS ONE THAT CAN BE REPRODUCED IN OTHERS

When is a leader convinced that he has reached a high level of leadership? When he has reproduced himself in others and is developing other leaders. As we will see later, this vision has a defined anointing of multiplication.

Those involved in the model of Twelve who work without sparing effort, will see compensation for their labor through the development of those and their team, who in turn will multiply the successful leader with the model of Twelve is one who shows solid fruit represented by those who have grown through his example, testimony, and teachings.

Chapter Seven

WHO IS WHO?

"Let your disciples draw from your spirit, this will raise their faith and the dexterity they need to achieve what you have." C.C.D.

PROFILE OF THE CANDIDATE TO THE TWELVE

The formation of the best team requires the selection of those with a specific profile. Every person who comes to the church is a potential leader. But only those with certain characteristics who meet a series of requirements for the development of the vision should be chosen. We cannot take disciples to a higher dimension then the one we have reached. We are their measuring rods of faith, and Christ's character inside us must be faithfully reproduced in them, so that they can reproduce it in others.

The leaders sets the guidelines and the pace at which the work will be accomplished, and the people around him should become familiar with, and accustomed to, the pace set before them. The team of twelve will be chosen after considering their best attributes. When my daughter Johanna wanted to form her group of Twelve she told my wife, "I need you to help me find people for my ministry." Her mother, who has always supported her in everything that she does, knew that that was Johanna's challenge, and told her that she had to accomplish this task on her own. In the next few months we were very pleased to see the way my daughter developed the Twelve without our help. Starting with a few, she did pastoral work, contacting people on the phone, making visitations, and investing personal time with them as if they were the most important people in the world. Sleepless nights, fasting and training were all necessary to arrive at the final selection of those who would be her Twelve. This took her about one year.

Selecting each one of the Twelve is as important as selecting your spouse. It requires time to get to know one another until you are absolutely certain that he or she is the right person. When the Lord chose His Twelve, He did so knowing that they would be with Him forever. The leader is a source of inspiration for those around him because with his experience he helps them to make the best use of their time.

The only way disciples are going to become skilled is by partaking of their leader's spirit. This heightens their faith and gives them the skills necessary to reach the maturity level of their leader.

Throughout my ministerial life I have learned that teamwork, multiplies our strength and generates powerful results. This is the reason I invest time with them. Thanks to our precious team we have been able to take big steps, such as moving the location of the church several times. Experience tells us that if a congregation moves more then ten blocks from its present location, it will loose thirty percent of its members. But as a team, we always triumph. Our members understand that the church is not the building. It's the people. Success in the cell system has become simple for many since we have made it our way of life.

Twelve pastors from the United Kingdom visited us. After an entire week of sharing experiences with different ones in the congregation, they told us, "What we have experienced here, we have not seen anywhere else in the world; all the people, from the youngest to the oldest speak the same language."

They marveled to see how each person achieved his goals. When my wife decided to lead the women's group, what impressed me most was the energy with which she directed the whole team. The reaction of the team was so positive that in a short time all the women in her group were of the same mind and thus caught the vision. In a few months they had organized and multiplied in a surprising way, and currently most of the women who make up her team have an average of 500 cells. Housewives, pastor's wives, businesswomen, widowed, form these teams and divorced women and they are all fruitful.

BE UNDER A BLESSING

If you desire to form a group of Twelve, you must see to it that your candidates have the ability to walk in the faith it takes to be recipients of the promises of God, and are thus able to release those blessings to others. This is God's desire for all His children. No one can give what he does not have, but if we are rich in the Lord, we can share this with others.

The same way that God set conditions in the garden of Eden for the first couple is how the Lord's blessings are conditioned upon us today. He says, "Son, if you want to enjoy My blessings, you must take from the fruit of the tree of life that is in My word. If you hear My word attentively and observe and practice it, it is as if you eat from the tree of life."

All the power of God's blessing for His children is found in His Word, and living under its precepts is to live under His blessing.

"Now it shall come to pass, if you diligently obey the voice of the Lord your God, to observe carefully all his commandments which I command you today, that the Lord your God will set you high above all nations of the earth." (Deuteronomy 28:1)

We are not only to hear His Word but also to observe and do all His commandments. When God says,"If you diligently obey the voice of the Lord," our senses are required to understand the Scriptures. There are two ways to fulfill the requirement of listening. First, when we scrutinize the Word we hear the voice of God, knowing that men of old spoke when inspired by the Holy Spirit, and the Bible is God's will revealed through the holy writers. The second way that we listen to God's voice is when He speaks to our hearts through the Holy Spirit. It is then that the necessity to do the will of the Lord is produced in us. It is important to point out that in the Bible we have the most accurate prophetic word, and prior to any sensation, the internal voice that we listen to must be subject to the Word of God. Anything inconsistent with the Bible cannot be accepted.

The great evangelist Smith Wigglesworth was known as the man of one book, because he purposed not to have contact with any other literature. His heart was so impregnated with the Word of God that practically every message that he spoke was prophetic.

One primary Characteristic to look for in our disciples is the intimate contact with the Bible so that they can live in its blessings. Listening to His voice and obeying His Word are characteristics of those with potential to be a candidate for our Twelve. Great servants of God spent hours in quietness and are then alert to God's voice consistent with the scriptures. This is when God brings specific texts to their minds to enlighten them.

BE A PERSON OF FAITH

The candidate of the Twelve must hear the voice of God, and observe to do it because, *"Moreover by them your servant is warned, and in keeping them there is great reward"* (Psalm 19:11). The Lord Jesus Christ gave us the best example of this when Satan was tempting Him. The Word He kept in his heart was used to counteract the evil attack.

"…having been built on the foundation of the apostles and prophets, Jesus Christ Himself being the chief cornerstone." (Ephesians 2:20)

The Word of God in our hearts is conducive to faith. The apostle Paul's goal was to develop the character of his disciple Timothy. Something that stood out in one of Paul's letters to him was his faith, which was an inheritance from his mother and grandmother. Acknowledging that faith comes by hearing, and hearing by the Word of God.

Each disciple who is in the process of development must learn to conquer in this realm of faith, to uncover the gifts and talents of a group of people ready to follow their leader. In the required steps of development requires a certain degree of faith.

Many who proudly show off their pastoral credentials have very few followers. When God calls someone to the pastorate, He bestows that privilege so that he can influence the development of other's lives. People of faith are sometimes compared to the eagle. When the mother eagle releases her eaglet in the air, he either opens his wings and flies in the air or crashes into the rocks below and dies. God deals with us in the same way; we either believe God and go after victory or we crash against the circumstances of life.

The apostle Paul said that the carnal mind cannot understand the things of the Spirit. To enter the realm of faith, one must have the mind of Christ, see things with eyes of faith, and not be influenced by circumstances. The man of faith learns to conquer everything in the Spiritual realm the he desires in the earthy realm, since the things of God are first spiritual. That's why he must learn to develop a great sensitivity to the things of the Spirit. Therefore, when God prompts him to do something he doesn't stop to think but acts immediately.

When Abraham was concerned whether his inheritance was going to be passed to his servant, God told him, *"This one shall not be your heir, but one who will come from your own body shall be your heir." Then God said, "Look now toward heaven, and count the stars if you are able to number them. So shall your descendants be"* (Genesis 15:4-5). Immediately Abraham started counting the stars in the sky ignoring his circumstances, though aware that Sarah his wife was old and infertile. But Abraham knew that when God said He would do something, He would do it.

Abraham understood the importance of giving faith to a dream and he spent hours watching the night stars looking at them as if he was looking in the faces of his descendants. Abraham believed in hope, and against hope, understanding that faith in God produces a hope completely opposite of natural reasoning. God took the patriarch through one of the most difficult journeys so that he could learn the power of faith. Men of God were not forged next to a sea contemplating seashells on the beach, but were faced with the greatest adversities, growing in God.

It is said of Moses, *"...for he endured as seeing Him who is invisible"* (Hebrews 11:27).

BE FULL OF VIRTUE

"...add to your faith virtue, to virtue knowledge..."
(2 Peter 1:5)

Jethro advised Moses, "Moreover you shall select from all the people able men, such as fear God. Men of faith, hating covetousness..." (Exodus 18:21)

Moses was to form a team of virtuous men. He was to look for the excellent men who developed their talents well and could therefore multiply themselves in others. Virtue is a special grace and ability to lead. It is what causes an athlete to run an excellent race, observing the rules and ranking the best. It is what causes a musician to excel in his art. It is known in the good leader and reflected in the team who follows him. The opposite of virtue or excellence is mediocrity. The candidate of the Twelve rejects conformity and always tries to do his best.

Virtue or excellence is an attribute of God expressed through the believer, and is a byproduct of a life of faith. Faith made Able a virtuous man and motivated him to give God an excellent offering. God enjoyed it so much that even after Abel's death, He was still talking about his offering. Faith made Noah a virtuous man and motivated him to build a great ship able to withstand the waters of The Flood. Powerful faith transformed Abraham into an extraordinary man and it allowed him to deposit his entire trust in the Lord.

We can create a parallel to the parable of the talents in terms of the cell vision: The man who had five cells multiplied them, but the man who had only one, after a year said, "Well, the truth is, the cell is still there." The Lord says, "Take away the cell form him and give it to the man who has ten." The arête (Greek for virtue) is the ability to multiply what has been entrusted to us.

Studying financiers, I was impressed by the way some of them work. I discovered information about a particular Korean who is known as the "Magician" because he has the ability to take a bankrupt corporation and transform it into a prosperous organization. This is an example of virtue. A virtuous person with an excellent spirit doesn't look at potential defeat, but only looks at how he can develop his vision and prosper it. The quality of virtue allows us to pick up defeated men and women and make them leaders of excellence. As previously noted, the first army David had was made up of men in debt, the distressed, and bitter of spirit. Nevertheless, God gave him the virtue to transform them to consolidate his kingdom.

BE KNOWLEDGEABLE OF THE TRUTH

Two common extremes exist in the Christian community: those who spend their entire lives filling their minds with theological knowledge but never reproduce it in others and those who want to spread the knowledge of the truth, but ignore it in their own lives. Both extremes are prejudicial. It is like a man who dedicated his whole life accumulating riches but never shared them with the needy because of his covetousness. Something similar happens to those who dedicate theirs lives acquiring biblical knowledge, and if they do not become doers of the Word of God, pride and arrogance soon follow. They begin to view others as poor immigrants and brag about the knowledge they have. A virtuous person is always enriching his life with the knowledge of the truth and pouring it into the lives of others. King Solomon said, "The substance of a diligent man is precious."

Acquiring knowledge of the truth often requires sacrifice of our time, dreams and often our own personal desires. But when that revelation knowledge comes, it produces great personal satisfaction. When you go to a supermarket, you don't take everything in sight but only those things you consider necessary, and that you select what your mind will consume. Solomon said that we should guard our minds like nothing else in the world. The knowledge of the truth will protect you from the corruption in this world.

Paul encouraged Timothy to occupy himself with reading, teaching, and exhortation. What kind of reading was the apostle referring to? I think that he was referring to literature that would contribute to biblical knowledge. It is our duty to help the group of Twelve grow not only in faith, but also in the knowledge of the Scriptures because faith comes by hearing the Word of God. That's why I usually select a number of books that I know are going to help in the development of their faith. Knowledge combined with practice makes us experts at handling the Word of God.

Furthermore, handling the Word of God is improved when the group of Twelve shares it with others because it requires effort and encourages them to demand more of themselves.

FEAR GOD AND EXERCISE SELF-CONTROL

"...able men, such as fear God, men of truth..."
(Exodus 18:21)

"...to knowledge self-control..." (2 Peter 1:6)

The fear of God must be established in all areas of our lives. Before entrusting someone with a great task, the Lord tests the heart. He determines whether or not we are faithful. Applying the principle that he who is faithful in the small things will be unfaithful with the increase.

One characteristic of someone who fears God is that he practices reverence that leads him to control his spirit. He takes all his desires to the cross, and dies to self everyday. He is someone who lives under the covenant of the blood of Christ, and like Paul lives under the covenant of the blood of Christ, and like Paul, can say, *"I have been crucified with Christ; it is no longer I who live, but Christ who lives in me; and the life which I now live in the flesh I live by faith of the Son of God"* (Galatians 2:20).

When we develop our people, we should guide them through disciplines that will help maintain self-control. This has motivated us to develop a program of fasting of fasting within the different ministries that make up our church. We start with 3 days of fasting, consuming only water. After a week of rest we do 7 days partial fasting, meaning one can eat only dinner. After another week of rest, 14 days of partial fasting are done. Another week of rest and then another 21 days of partial fasting are done. After another week of rest, the last period of 40 days of partial fasting completes the program. Generally during this time of fasting, we pray specifically for the group's established goals to be achieved.

Self-control produces the fear of God, and he who lives in that fear abstains from sinning because he doesn't want to offend God in the least.

ABHOR COVETOUSNESS

Paul warned Timothy, *"For the love of money is the root of all kinds of evil..."* (1 Timothy 6:10). Nothing can destroy a leader more than when he allows the things of this world to have a place in his heart. Idolatry consists of placing one's trust in anything outside of God. Unfortunately, there are many who have allowed themselves, to be seduced by money.

In recounting the first battle of Ai, this was a period in time when Israel trusted in God. After having seen the impressive walls of Jericho fall like a card castle, the fear of God had fallen on all of them. But one man, Achan, brought defeat to the entire nation in this battle by persuading the children of Israel to steal the loot from Jericho and bury it. The silver and gold were kept back, not to enrich the people but to beautify the tabernacle and its services. God's desire and lesson in all of this was to keep the people's faith and religion uncontaminated. He did not want the loot to remind Israel of the Canaanite practices that influenced them. But once the sin was recognized and punished, God told Joshua to take heart and try again. This time the city of Ai was taken.

We see how Achan, unable to appreciate the consequences of his actions, was moved by a spirit of covetousness and allowed himself to be seduced by the things he knew were cursed. The power of the curse in those objects affected the military performance of Israel when they went off to face their enemies and they were greatly defeated. In order to remove the evil from the midst of the people, Achan and his family had to die, and his possessions destroyed, as well as the stolen objects.

Covetousness brought deadly consequences to this man and his entire household. Solomon said, "...*so a curse without cause shall not alight*" (Proverbs 26:2).

Judas tried to disguise covetousness behind a spirit of compassion. When the woman poured perfume of alabaster on His feet, Judas told the Lord, "What a waste, why wasn't this perfume sold for thirty denarius and given to the poor instead?" He said this not because he cared for the poor but because he was greedy. He was also in charge of the money and was stealing from the treasury. The leader must discern who in his group may have a spirit of greed and supervise him until that person is free of that demonic influence.

Chapter Eight

YOU ARE THE LEADER

"Whoever cultivates friendship with the Holy Spirit develops a level of supernatural authority that allows him to rise above circumstances." C.C.D.

ATTRIBUTES THAT DISTINGUISH A LEADER OF TWELVE

As we saw in the previous chapter, the candidate of a team of Twelve must meet certain requirements, while at the same time have acquired the ability to lead a group of Twelve and possess the attributes to guide others.

Jesus' prayer for His disciples gives us the framework for such attributes. In it the Lord expresses the way He developed His Team.

"I have manifested Your name to man whom You have given Me out of the world. They were Yours, You gave them to Me, and they have kept Your word." (John 17:6)

The Lord knew the Twelve were not His, but the Father's. And through intercessory prayer all night, He convinced the Father to entrust them to Him. That's why He says, "They were Yours, and You gave them to me." Once they started to come to Him, He taught them the knowledge of the Father and enjoyed seeing the way they received the Word with gladness and obeyed it. The following are attributes of a leader.

HE IS RECOGNIZED BY HIS TEAM
AS A PERSON OF FAITH

"Now they have known that all things which you have given me are from You." (John 17:7)

Jesus' disciples recognized that he totally depended on God, and in ministry to others, they saw how He moved in faith. They in turn worked with Him on many occasions. It is important for each person being discipled to trust his leader. The leader's testimony gives them, the assurance, that they truly are men and women of faith, and that they operate in the supernatural as Jesus did.

HE IS FAITHFUL TO THE MESSAGE
THAT HE COMMUNICATES

'*For I have given them the words which You have given Me; and they have received them, and have known surely that I came forth from You; and they have believed that You sent me."* (John 17:8)

The leader must be faithful to the message he communicates to his Twelve. He should not preach his own philosophy, but should let them know what he has received from God. The leader doesn't communicate his own vision, but respects the line of authority that comes from God. This respect and fidelity brings peace and security to his Twelve.

HE ALWAYS PRAYS FOR HIS DISCIPLES

"I pray for them. I do not pray for the world but for those whom You have given Me, for they are Yours." (John 17:9)

The leader always takes care of the team in prayer. Many limit their devotional time interceding for the sick or those in bondage to a vice and never include their disciples or leaders in their prayers. The leader must raise a wall of protection of prayer around his Twelve.

HE IS HONORED BY THE FRUIT OF HIS TWELVE

"And all Mine are Yours, and Yours are Mine and I am glorified in them." (John 17:10)

As the group matures and bears fruit, they begin to raise their leader to a position of respect and greatness. That's why Jesus said, " I am glorified in them." The fruit of the disciples is a guarantee that Divine riches are given to the leader.

HE LIVES IN THE SUPERNATURAL

"Now I am no longer in the world, but these are in the world, and I come to You. Holy Father, keep through Your name those whom You have given me, that they may be one as We are." John 17:11

The leader does not live according to the dictates of this world. He develops an authority level that passes from the natural realm to the supernatural. The person who lives in the natural realm acts according to his circumstances, but the one who lives in the super natural acts above his circumstances.

When the leader acts in the supernatural realm he develops authority over principalities, powers, and the rulers of the darkness of this world. He possesses the gift of discernment of spirits and moves in a dimension of faith. This authority allows him to know the weaknesses of his Twelve and he implores the Lord in faith to help them to overcome. He drives away evil from his team, establishing unity, that they may be one as we are one. The group must always strengthen their ties of unity until this characteristic reaches maturity.

HE PROTECTS HIS TWELVE

"While I was with them in the world, I kept them in Your name. Those whom you gave me I have kept; and none of them is lost except the son of perdition, that the scripture might be fulfilled." (John 17:12)

How does the leader keep or protect his Twelve? In prayer, ministering to them, discerning their needs, and supporting them emotionally, as well as materially.

HE IMPARTS TEACHINGS THAT REMAIN

"But now come I to You, and these things I speak in the world, that they may have my joy fulfilled in themselves." (John 17:13)

The first part of this verse makes reference to the absence of the leader. But after he imparts eternal truth, the teachings will endure and produce joy in the hearts of the Twelve. In 1997, I decided to cancel all engagements outside of Colombia and stay in church. But when the murder attempt on my life occurred, the Lord told me to live outside of the country for a few months.

When I talked to the leaders about the decision, they told me, "Don't worry pastor, we'll keep working the vision and fulfilling our goals." The teachings they previously received challenged them and imparted joy and motivation to carry out their objectives, and all the time I was absent, they duplicated their efforts, and in unity developed excellent results.

HE IS DILIGENT IN THE
FORMATION OF HIS TWELVE

"I have given them Your word; and the world has hated them because they are not of the world, just as I am not of the world." (John 17:14)

The formation of the twelve is set in three stages. The first corresponds to the spiritual "baby" who receives unadulterated milk in discipleship.

The second is when the Twelve have shown signs of maturity and can receive bread or solid food. This is the stage of education in the School of leaders and is the food that will strengthen them in adversity.

The third is when the Twelve are on a higher level of spiritual maturity and rise above their circumstances. They receive more intense development that allows them to counteract the enemy and go on the spiritual offensive because they have learned to overcome trials. Trials measure the caliber of the leader.

HE STRENGTHENS HIS TWELVE

"I do not pray that You should take them out of the world, but that You should keep them from the evil one."
(John 17:15)

The leader of Twelve is always praying to the Lord for victory to defeat the temptations of the world. Again, he prays for Divine protection so that his team is kept from evil.

Although they have grown in their Christian life, the leader does not let go of them in prayer at any time.

HE IS CONFIDENT OF THE
CONDUCT OF HIS DISCIPLES

"They are not of the world, just as I am not of the world." (John 17:16)

This expression appears twice in John's prayer in chapter 17. In the first, the disciple had not yet defeated evil, and in the second, they had overcome it.

When Jesus went to the desert and fasted 40 days, he was tempted by the adversary but faced him because He had the anointing to do it. The anointing comes in stages. When Jesus defeated temptation, a greater anointing of the Holy Spirit rested on Him.

When a disciple defeats evil, he is covered with a greater authority, and this is something the leader must inculcate in each disciple.

HE PREPARES HIS TWELVE FOR
THE ANOINTING OF SANCTITY

"Sanctify them by Your truth. Your word is truth." (John 17:17)

Sanctification allows the disciple to clearly know the truth, deepening his study of the Word of God and the preparation for this is the leader's responsibility. When one defeats evil, sanctification is received and this anointing allows for the illumination of the truth.

HE USES EACH SITUATION TO
TEACH HIS TWELVE

"For I have given to them the words which You have given Me; and they have received them..." (John 17:8a)

There wasn't a moment the Lord didn't take the opportunity to impart His doctrine to His Twelve. He enabled them so that they could achieve with precision the mission He had entrusted them, and this motivated Him even amidst diverse kinds of circumstances. He left lessons for His team even in the smallest details of life. On one occasion He took them to the temple, to teach them about giving and said, "Look at how each one gives the offering." Afterwards, He asked what they had observed. Perhaps some said, "Lord, some people are very generous, like those who deposited large amounts of money; such generosity!" He essentially replied, "Don't be fooled they gave their leftovers, but their offering will not be taken into account. Now, what do you think about the widow's offering?" Perhaps one of the disciples criticized the small offering of the widow, who gave only a few coins. But Jesus taught them not to be fooled here. She gave more because she gave everything that she had. The Twelve never forgot the lesson that the offering that pleases God, is that which comes from a pure heart.

Jesus was reproducing His vision and his spirit in the Twelve men, and they continually drank from His never ending Source. The anointing was transmitted simply by living amongst the people and by walking alongside the Lord. Each of them was so close to Him that when Peter later denied the Lord, he tried being inconspicuous, but was recognized as one of Jesus' disciples. It was impossible for him to hide behind his denial, and while he tried to pass as someone else, he couldn't because he has the Master's anointing. There is a great difference in the way Jesus related to his disciples, and the way many spiritual leaders today relate to their disciples.

HE PREPARES HIS TEAM FOR EVANGELISTIC WORK

"As You sent me into the world, I also have sent them into the world." (John 17:18)

The leader must prepare his Twelve to develop the vision through evangelistic work. The vision is reproduced when the disciples defeat the evil one and enter a life of sanctification. This is when the Scriptures open up to their understanding and they are sent into the world to reproduce.

HE ABIDES IN SANCTIFICATION

"And for their sakes I sanctify Myself, that they also might be sanctified by the truth." (John 17:19)

Sanctification is a command of God to each one of His children. He said, *"Be holy, because I am holy."* God desires for us to fellowship and worship Him, and to elevate our lives to His standard of holiness. He would never ask us to do something we couldn't achieve. The leader knows that keeping himself sanctified, will serve to inspire his Twelve to do the same. In this way the vision will be honored in their personal witness.

HE PRAYS FOR THE TWELVE OF HIS TWELVE

"I do not pray for these alone, but also for those who will believe in Me through their word." (John 17:20)

In addition to praying continually for his basic team, the leader dedicates time to pray for the disciples of their group of Twelve.

Every leader of twelve must intercede for his 144, those who are the fruit of each one of the members of his main team. He also prays for the 1,728 that are the Twelve of each one of the 144.

In the days of the apostles, the deacons were established to serve in the church because the apostles did not want to be distracted by serving tables, but dedicated their efforts to praying and studying the Word. That is the job of the leader today.

This type of praying helps to maintain unity and promotes the anointing received from the Father, as seen in the verse below.

"And the glory which You gave me I have given them, that they may be one just as We are one." (John 17:22)

HE REPRODUCES HIS CHARACTER
IN HIS TWELVE

By transferring His Spirit, the Lord was giving His own life to His team. Like seed sown in the earth, it produces corresponding fruit. Jesus invested his life in His disciples because He considered them to be good soil. Therefore, it was logical that they would produce Christ's character in their lives. A question arises: Why wasn't the Master's character reproduced in Judas' life? It was because his heart already had an owner, the love of money. Jesus said that you cannot serve two lords at the same time because you will love one and hate the other. You cannot serve both God and riches.

Anyone who does not place his full allegiance in the Lord is not adequately prepared to have his life cultivated. Full surrender is necessary. This is why Jesus dedicated three-and-a-half years of His life to the development of character in his apostles and later breathed His Spirit into them. Each disciple who is training in a leadership position must continually stay in Christ's presence through the reading of the Word so that the Holy Spirit can nurture and mature him. He must motivate others to do the same.

HE WORKS TOWARDS UNITY

"I in them, and You in me; that they may be made perfect in one, and that the world may know that You have sent Me, and have loved them as You have loved Me." (John 17:23)

The leader knows that perfect unity comes as a result of a relationship with the Holy Spirit. The ones being mentored are not just another head in the conglomerate but are an active part of a living spiritual organism, the body of Christ. When great respect for authority exists it produces an influential testimony before the world. Jesus said, in reference to His Father, "…that the world may know that You sent me." This kind of unity encourages the Twelve and establishes in their hearts that God loves them as he loves their leader.

At times members of a team of Twelve may struggle in one way or another to get their leader's attention. If he doesn't give them the attention that they need, they will feel rejected and experience a lack of love. However, a disciple who has matured spiritually knows that he is loved. He feels worthy and accepted, and together they enjoy the love of God and the love of each other.

HE FORMS A TEAM FOR LIFE

"Father, I desire that they also whom You gave Me may be with Me where I am, that they may behold My glory which You have given me; for You loved Me before the foundation of the world." (John 17:24)

Jesus teaches that the Twelve are for life. Through the leader, God removes the veil of limitation off the Twelve and lets them see the faith of the one who leads them and the anointing they have received from him. "That they also whom You gave Me may be with Me where I am." In the ministry, we go through many different stages, yet it doesn't matter how many stages we pass through, the Twelve are always going to be with us.

In the same way that a person enters a marriage covenant and becomes sure of the one with whom he is going to spend the rest of his life, so it is with the group of Twelve. In the story of Ruth, her mother-in-law Naomi tried to persuade her to return to her land and her gods, but she pleaded, *"Entreat me not to leave you, or turn back from following after you; for wherever you go, I will go; and wherever you lodge, I will lodge; your people shall by my people, and your God, my God. Where you die, I will die, and there will I be buried. The Lord do so to me, and more also, if anything but death parts you and me"* (Ruth 1:16-17).

Ruth's covenant with Naomi was a covenant of faithfulness to death. God honored her for this. She later became King David's great-grandmother.

The faithfulness of the apostles was so sure that the Lord tested it in different ways. With the exception of Judas, they all remained faithful. That's why the Lord asked in prayer that they remain with Him in the place prepared by the Father. Such was the commitment of these Twelve that after Jesus left this world they were prepared to face any adversity out of love for Him.

HE IS SURE OF THEIR SPIRITUAL CONDITION

"O righteous Father! The world has not known You, but I have known You; and these have known that You sent me." (John 17:25)

The leader knows the vision that God has given him, will not be understood by those who remain in the carnal realm. The Bible says that the natural man does not understand the things of the Spirit because they must be spiritually discerned. The mind of the leader and his disciples is opened through a delegation of authority that makes the vision clear, while recognizing that such a vision comes from God.

When the apostles devised a defense before the members of Jerusalem's council, Peter, filled with the Holy Spirit, declared, *"This is the stone which was rejected by you builders, which has become the chief cornerstone. Nor is there salvation in any other, for there is no other name under heaven given among men by which we must be saved"* (Acts 4:11-12).

The apostles knew their leader very well and they gladly defended His name. Later, the members of the council tried to intimidate the apostles to try to prevent them from speaking to anybody in the name of Jesus. But they responded, *"...Whether it is right in the sight of God to listen to you more than God, you judge. For we cannot but speak the things which we have seen and heard"* (Acts 4:19-20).

They knew the desire of the Lord's heart was to preach to the lost, so they remained faithful to the message wherever they went. Even though they knew that they risked being flogged, jailed, and even put to death, they did not deny their faith in Jesus in order to fulfill their calling.

HE DOESN'T STOP GUIDING THEM
IN THE KNOWLEDGE OF THE LORD

"And I have declared to them Your name, and will declare it..." (John 17:26)

Most of the Jews resisted accepting Jesus as Lord, because they accepted their redeemer to be a great political leader who would liberate them from the yoke of the Roman Empire. When they saw Jesus associate with societies less fortunate, they couldn't conceive that the awaited Messiah would be associating with the poor or the beggars and sinners. They thought, If this man keeps leading in this way the Romans would come and overrun us. That's why they always presented arguments to question His validity and challenge His authority. *"He came to his own, and His own did not receive Him. But as many as received Him, to them He gave the right to become children of God, to those who believe in His name"* (John 1:11-12).

The Jews were blessed to be instruments of God so that salvation could come through them. But because of a capricious attitude, they discarded the opportunity. That's why the Lord opened doors so that even the Gentiles would have the opportunity to partake of this precious salvation.

HE DEVELOPS THE MATURITY OF THE TEAM IN LOVE

"...that the love with which You loved me may be in them, and I in them."(John 17:26b)

The strength of God's love is clearly revealed in His willingness to undergo extreme suffering to rescue the object of His love: mankind. Therefore My Father loves me, because I lay down My life that I might take it again. No one takes it from Me, but I lay it down of Myself. I have power to lay it down, and I have power to take it again. This command I have received of my father" (John 10:17-18). His love was demonstrated through His works, He died to redeem His own people. However He, said, "No one takes it from Me, but I lay it down of Myself."

In genuine love, there is a total and unconditional surrender for the mission that God has entrusted us. The leader desires that his team reach a level of maturity in sincere love, i.e., agape, which comes from God and grows in their hearts. This is the level of love that motivates the members of the team to defend the cause of Christ, just as the Lord's disciples were ready to do when they matured spiritually. At first Peter denied the Lord, but when he matured, he was ready to lay down his life for Him. The strength of godly love will always be expressed, as it was through Jesus, in sacrificial acts of giving.

Are you ready to form your team of Twelve? Remember, all things are possible if your answer is affirmative, then you are the leader.

Chapter Nine

THE TICK-TOCK OF THE CLOCK

"Each battle won is the result of a leader who knew how to strategically place his people." C.C.D.

ALL ELEMENTS OF THE VISION ARE INDISPENSABLE

The success of the vision of the Twelve depends on the precise elements from which it is made up. Each step is necessary to achieve the next, until the end result is reached which will guide our mission to win the world for Christ. Like a clock the sound indicates the precision that allows for accurate performance, the vision is also a system made up of essential pieces, that when adequately applied, leads to success.

PRECISION, AFFINITY AND EFFECTIVENESS

One of the most popular tourist attractions known the world over is London's Big Ben Tower. The popular appeal isn't the tower itself but the clock. It is considered the most synchronized and precise clock in the world, such that in every country, adjustments are made daily to their official times using Big Ben as the reference. Although there is a time differential because of geography, nevertheless countries take into account the time of this particular clock to achieve precision in knowing the actual time in their respective regions.

Investigating the functioning of this famous clock, we discovered that it is the object of continuous maintenance. Each one of its parts is examined so that they remain adjusted to the others. Those who are in charge of the delicate work, use the sound, produced by the mechanism, when the clock's hands move, its tick-tock, confirms if the clock is working properly. It may be surprising to know that a sound often gone unnoticed by ordinary people can indicate, to the trained ear, the correct or incorrect functioning of the whole apparatus. When something goes wrong with Big Ben, for example, where a part may be damaged, its characteristic tick-tock changes. Immediately maintenance is performed so that the exact time remains accurate and is not adversely effected.

BIG BEN AND THE PRINCIPLE OF THE TWELVE

Big Ben and Swiss watches might sound interesting, but what do they have to do with our vision? While at a convention with some leaders, I was looking for a way to illustrate the effectiveness of the vision. The words synchronization came to mind in the need to keep all elements of the model in harmony so that planned objectives are achieved.

"The clock has a device that generates a base of time, a system that parting from that base, defines the hour to be indicated, and a setting device. The setting of time is carried out through an analogue (Moving hands) or digital (Fixed numerals set through electro-luminescent diodes or liquid crystals) device."

When I learned about the functioning mechanism of a clock, I concluded: Our vision has a mechanism, a system or device called principle of Twelve. This system generates a base to achieve goals, and from this base (the Twelve) the objective to be achieved is indicated in reference to growth and multiplication. The setting of that multiplication goal is done through an analogue device or strategy (moving hands to win lost souls) that we call homogenous groups.

The vision is then a system comparable to the mechanism of a clock. The face is not the most important part but only serves for orientation, because it has the number outlined with the four principle times. What is really important is the machinery that determines its functioning, and this is precisely what is not seen. In the vision we see a face, observed by everyone, but behind it there is a mechanical organization that maintains clockwork order. It's a hazard to get distracted by the face and its twelve numbers while the machinery lies "rusting". In other words, if leaders are incapacitated and cannot perform because they are constrained by bondages, the system cannot work and the gears don't move. That's why it's important to ensure all members of the team understand the vision in order to take it to others nations.

In this way, the "clock's accurate movement" of their model of Twelve is achieved when different pieces comprising each team member are likeminded in their objective. This vision is an integral system and all individual factors are essential in developing groups of Twelve. It is not enough to win people, it is also necessary to consolidate the fruit and to disciple the new believer in his spiritual development. However, we cannot limit ourselves to discipleship, it is also necessary for the individual to be sent to multiply his mentor's efforts by reproducing Christ's character in others. The vision's essential steps will be explained thoroughly in the third section of this book.

Returning to the formation and structure of the Twelve, the three vital aspects are made up of the pre-encounter, encounter and post-encounter. The group work habits, relationships and precision of this system is determined by each step through which men and women must pass until they mature into group leaders.

ADJUSTING THE VISION'S CLOCKWORK THROUGH HOMOGENOUS GROUPS

There are times when leaders act prematurely in the formation of their groups of Twelve, impulsively wanting to achieve their objectives. When examining why results are not optimal. They discover that in their groups there may be a mix of professionals, non- professionals, and even students and housewives. We do not discriminate, but whenever possible, the leader must establish traits of harmony and agreement so that the entire team works together towards common objectives there is no doubt that the model of Twelve values the contribution of each member in spiritually homogenous cells, and we, in fact, have cell groups formed by both professionals and housewives, and their growth has been phenomenal.

It is important to note that in the selection of the Twelve our first choice will not always be the optimal "piece" to fit in our clock, but our work must continue in developing the character of each member until he reaches expected levels of growth. The objective is to get the clock to run accurately.

As one can see, this is a well-defined model, whose precision guaranties the reaping of extraordinary fruit, when each member is properly cared for.

"For as the body is one and has many members, but all members of that body, being many, are one body, so also is Christ...And God has appointed these in the church: first apostles, second prophets, third teachers, after that miracles, then gifts of healings, helps, administrations, varieties of tongues." (1 Corinthians 12:12, 28)

This biblical reference emphasizes the importance of the homogeneity of the groups of twelve. This has contributed to the vision expanding widely and quickly, both inside and outside of Colombia in homogenous groups, the gifts are easily detected and the disciple who possesses them starts defiling himself as a potential leader. Our experience shows that homogenous groups are a part of a strategy which guarantees harmonious and accelerated growth. Since we have implemented this aspect of the vision, multiplication has grown in such a way that our statistical projections are continually exceeded.

The Twelve must develop their work in a homogeneous setting: let a young person win another young person, a man win another man, a woman win another woman, a couple win another couple, and children win other children. At one time we started by dividing the city in zones, as Pastor Cho does in Korea. We divided the city in 20 zones (using electoral districts) but this mechanism didn't work. The fruit demonstrated by Pastor Cho is extraordinary, but our cultural context operates differently. We found that people lost their commitment, and leaders in each zone struggled to stay with people in their electoral districts. Cell growth dropped and we had to look for a mechanism to correct this and overcome it. That's how the idea of homogeneous groups was developed. We started to implement this in the central church, and in only one year, this location equaled the number of cells in all the other zones combined. With the homogeneous group mechanism, our subdivision discussions ended and growth improved wonderfully.

VISION OF UNITY AND MINISTERIAL IDENTITY

Why does homogenization produce vast results? Because a social principle teaches that, "Common elements of individuals cause them to gravitate to each other and stay in cohesion and unity." Homogeneity and identification allows for the development of the community. The church should not discard the advantages of this system. When transferring these concepts to work in the vision of Twelve, its viability allows for firm and accelerated growth, forming groups identified by something in common; age, sex, profession, et cetera. All receive the same gospel, the same doctrine, the same principles of leadership, and consequently, the same guidelines to interrelate with the vision and contribute to the achievement of its goals. By definition, homogeneous groups are: Clusters of people grouped together by common interests, in search of the same objectives, and with the tendency to satisfy the same needs, while always trying to develop the vision of the church.

The impact and far reaching effect of homogeneous groups is practically incalculable and has been so since their formation. We have proven that the penetration of society with the gospel, by this means, is faster and more efficient. We can say, unequivocally, that with homogeneous groups there are no social, educational, or economic limits that hinder the fulfillment of the Great Commission through the preaching of the Word of God.

The growth of the church that the Lord has allowed my wife Claudia and I to shepherd, is due to homogeneous groups, in the total perspective of the vision. Day after day, each new believer who comes to church anxious to know more about the Word of God, satisfies his expectations and pacifies his anxiety when he finds his group in church with which he identifies through age, sex, or martial status. A person, who comes to church with problems of a spiritual or emotional nature, immediately notices that when placed in the correct group, members identify with his problems and help to solve them with practical solutions from the Scriptures and guidance from the Holy Spirit. It is because they speak the same language, have the same perspectives, and all work toward the same objective, the Divine vision.

From any viewpoint, homogeneous groups are the best strategies a church can employ if it desires unprecedented growth, the anointing of God, with established healthy doctrine that will never allow the church to fail. This is what we have proven in our experience. Homogeneous groups have functionality so strategic that they never allow a new believer to feel out of place in relation to the vision. Furthermore, one who is born again finds a solid group of like-minded people with whom he is compatible and remains there. Soon he sees himself as a useful member and feels that his presence is important to the rest of the group. This is the same regardless of the age group to which the newcomer belongs. The secret of homogeneous groups is the existence of common factors that facilitates the gathering of people within the group.

These groups initially surfaced in our church with young people in 1989. While they established common identity they all desired to achieve the development of the church's vision. It is a commitment in which each member contributes his small part and receives the satisfaction of being part of a spiritual revival in which Columbia shines as an example for the world.

The homogeneous groups we have are: the youth, who constitute an important bastion of growth, each assembling 18,000 at El Campin Coliseum in Bogotá; the men's net, which exalts the priesthood of man in the family and in social leadership; the women's net, which reflects the role of women in the vision that transcends national boundaries; the couple's ministry emphasizes matrimonial life within the growth perspective of the church that greatly benefits our families; finally the ministry of the children, with which the effectiveness of the vision is observed while preparing new generations.

There is something common in all these groups. While they associate by age, sex, and other affinities according to the role they perform, collectively they are identified by their cell group commitment and their preparation for leadership. When homogeneous groups develop and mature, dynamism emanates from the anointing of the Holy Spirit as a protagonist of the cell multiplying process. This has an effect on the whole church. In the homogeneous groups the manifestation of the Spirit has been given to each one for their benefit, according to. (1 Corinthians 12:7)

The need for the leader to be a living example of Christ with a spotless testimony is very important for his ministry's success. At the international Charismatic Mission we understand this well, that's why the spiritual and numerical results have only increased in our homogeneous groups.

Chapter Ten

EQUIPPED FOR TRIUMPH

"The anointing of God equips all to triumph. Faith inspires us, love sustains us, but only perseverance will take us to the end." C.C.D.

THE INTEGRAL FORMATION OF THE TEAM OF TWELVE

It is not enough to select your team. Choosing your Twelve is only the first part of a process that culminates when each one is discipled and equipped.

Practically speaking, each person arrives, in the rough and needs a spiritual polisher to break off curses, release bonds of afflictions, deliver from oppression, heal wounds, and teach doctrinal principles regarding the vision.

A HEALTHY LEADER CAN BE USED TO HEAL OTHERS

No respected technical coach would send one of his athletes to compete in an important race with his feet full of sores. In that condition he would completely fail. The same applies to ministry. If we aspire to a solid ministry and want to achieve high expectations, all members of the Twelve must pass through a process of rebuilding, including healing of the soul. When God created us, He made us tripartite beings, spirit, soul and body. In the soul we find the mind, will and emotions. Most people have been wounded in their emotions, and if they have never dealt with these wounds, in most cases they raise an impenetrable barrier before others, implying, "I was wounded once, I will not risk being wounded again."

I count on the support of pastors who move in the supernatural. They understand and minister very well in he healing of the soul and in deliverance, but that know that they personally must be open to a much deeper ministry that God by his Spirit may want to perform.

I am reminded of a meeting where such ministry had taken place. After sharing the Word of God we had a time of prayer. I could hear rending screams from some of the men of this group. For the first time, many of them opened their hearts before God, and with His help faced their bitter past experiences. When we listened to their testimonies, one of them said, "The night before my twelfth birthday, my father had received my report card, and because my grades were not that good, his present to me was a thorough beating, from that day, it has been difficult for me to relate to authority, because I always associate it with my father. Even though he is deceased, I have not been able to forgive him." At that moment I stood up approached him and took his father's place, and told him, "Son, forgive me for I was so unfair to you in how I responded concerning your grades, and not for celebrating your birthday. Son, forgive my ignorance." After I made this repentance he began to moan indescribably, causing the whole group to tremble. Immediately, everyone experienced a breakthrough, and liberty was released in many.

Later, after the meeting each shared their personal experiences of knowing God as their true Father. Months later, the wives of this group commended on the way God totally transformed the lives of these pastors. This historic meeting proved to be a milestone in their Christian lives.

WE POSSESS AN ETERNAL NATURE

To be part of the Twelve is more than just participating in formal meetings with your leader, of having status in your community. Being part of the Twelve is to realize we are sons of God and therefore possess an eternal nature. All who have accepted Jesus as their Savior have a Divine nature, because God's spirit imparts that spiritual nature in each of us. Furthermore each one has the same authority Jesus had while on Earth, since he too is as son of God. " *He came to his, and His own did not receive Him. But as many as received Him, to them He gave the right to become children of God, to those who believe in His name: who were born, not of blood, nor of the will of the flesh, nor of the will of man, but of God*" (John 1:11-13).

AUTHORITY OVER DEMONS

Different forms of life exist in God's creation. The lowest life form is in the mineral kingdom, followed by the animal kingdom, and then human beings. Above man is the angelic order, and the highest form is life in God's kingdom. Angelic hosts belong to that kingdom, but for the rebellion of one chief angel, known as the Morning Star, came one of the most violent of God's trials He cast Lucifer and one third of the angels out of heaven, leaving them in an inferior position in relation to angels who stayed faithful to God. We know them today as Satan and the angelic hordes as demons.

After this incident came the creation of man. Satan cunningly used a creature of the animal kingdom to deceive earth's first couple, and in so doing all authority God had given the first couple was transferred to Satan's rebellious angelic order. This left the human race, lower in authority then them but when Christ came into this world, He confronted Satan's kingdom.

Throwing a mortal dart at Jesus on Calvary's cross, Satan thought that he was forever getting rid of Jesus. But Jesus knew that Cavalry meant man's deliverance from demonic oppression. It was Satan's greatest defeat. Although Satan knows of his defeat brought about by Jesus, he fights to keep man ignorant of this truth so that he may continue exercising control over him. The enemy knows that the moment people discover the truth; it will set them free and will elevate them to the highest level of life in the kingdom of God.

After the Lord's resurrection from the dead, He ascended into heaven and sat at the right hand of the Majesty and all was subordinate at His feet. *"He was, far above all principality and power and might and dominion, and every name that is named, not only in this age but also in which is to come. And He put all things under His feet..."* (Ephesians 1:21-22). The Lord took back from the adversary all power he had over humanity. St. Paul said, *"And raised us up together, and made us sit together in the heavenly places in Christ Jesus"* (Ephesians 2:6).

AUTHORITY OVER THE CURSE

"Like a flitting sparrow, like a flying swallow, so a curse without cause shall not alight." (Proverbs 26:2)

God has spoken of blessings that chase us until they catch up with us. "*Surely goodness and Mercy shall follow me all the days of my life…*" (Psalms 23:6). What does this mean? It means that to receive a blessing, God first has to test your heart to see if you really live your life according to his Word and if you do, God commands blessings to chase you until they catch you.

On the other hand, the writer of Proverbs says that curses always happen for a reason, and many know that evil is chasing them but don't know how to break that which binds them.

Every believer must know that in the world we are in a declared war against forces of evil, and that this battle functions through arguments and vain imaginations that human beings allow due to mistakes of their past. That's why curses have power and authority over individuals or entire families. There is no doubt that the American Kennedy clan has been followed by the shadow of a curse, which doesn't allow members of that family to fully develop, but ensnares them no matter what station in life they reach. Riches, fame, or good friends do not cure a curse. The only thing that defeats a curse is the power of the blood of the Lamb. "*And they overcame him by the blood of the lamb and by the word of their testimony, and they did not love their lives to the death*" (Revelation 12:11). When we compare blessings and curses, we notice that blessings are powerful, but so are curses.

Two opposite sides exist; good exists, but evil exists too. God traced our path ahead of us in order for us to walk in blessing. But He also tells us that there is a path that can take us to the curse, and many have stepped on the enemy's terrain.

Solomon said, "There is something that motivates the birds to fly, something that motivates the swallow, just as there is something that motivates the curse." The curse doesn't come by chance; it enters when someone opens the door to it. But thank God that Scriptures teach that all arguments against us were already cancelled through the redemptive work of the cross, "*...having wiped out the handwriting of requirements that was against us, which was contrary to us. And He has taken it out of the way, having nailed it to the cross.*" (Colossians 2:14).

THE ANOINTING IS REPRODUCED ON CONTACT

"*And when He had called His twelve disciples to him, He gave them power over unclean spirits, to cast them out, and to heal all kinds of sickness and all kinds of disease.*" (Matthew 10:1)

Jesus invested three-and -a –half years of His life reproducing his anointing in His twelve. He developed a first class team, and each one moved in the same dimension of faith as their Lord. They were accustomed to seeing the Lord perform miracles, but doing the same miracles without the Lord present was another thing. Jesus had given them the anointing to cast out demons and heal the sick, now it was their turn to believe Him and start moving in the same dimension of faith. When they came back with their report, they were joyful to report that even demons were subject to them in His name, "*Nevertheless do not rejoice in this, that the spirits are subject to you, but rather rejoice because your names are written in heaven*" (Luke 10:20).

Years ago I suggested to my team of pastors to program miracle services in their respective churches. I pointed out that they already possessed the anointing and all they had to do was to act in faith. It was a great challenge because they were used to me, as Pastor, doing the ministry for the people.

That Sunday they prayed: "Lord, let the sick come today who have head or stomach aches, but don't send us any difficult cases." One of them later said that he asked the first sick person, "What are you sick of?" He answered, "Cancer." The needs of most of the sick that came were similar serious cases. But when they prayed for them, they were indeed surprised seeing how the Lord moved performing all kinds of miracles on the sick. *"And these signs will follow those who believe: In my name they will cast out demons; they will speak with new tongues; they will take up serpents; and if they drink anything deadly, it will by no means hurt them; they will lay hands on the sick, and they will recover"* (Mark 16:17-18).

The Lord continually transmitted His anointing to His Twelve. Scripture says that even the shadow of Peter ministered healing to the sick. As leaders, we must transmit the master's anointing and authority to each member of our team so that they can minister effectively to others.

Chapter Eleven

DEVELOP THE VISION OF THE TWELVE

"Each disciple is a potential leader and will become what we have sown in him." C.C.D.

EFFECTIVE GUIDELINES FOR SUCCESS

I expect that up to now, you have received sufficient motivation to desire to make this type of success apart of your own life. What God has given me in this vision has, up to this day, been extremely successful and I continue to share it with the world.

I trust it will be much more successful for other believers, leaders, and pastors like you, as you set out to develop it. If that is your goal, the following guidelines will be very helpful to get the vision of the Twelve up and running.

BREAK THE SCHEMES

To implement the model of Twelve requires abandoning traditional methods and embarking on a totally different way. Growth is guaranteed if it is approached in faith. Don't act like those who want to take the easy road trying to adopt a little from here and a little from there, thinking that if they take the best of the Korean model, the best of the El Salvadorian model, the best of the Honduran model, and the best of the Columbian model, they will have the perfect model.

This will never work because the model of Twelve is very specialized, you either embrace it entirely or you do not, there is no middle ground for compromise.

DIG DEEP TO LAY FOUNDATIONS

Our Lord recognized that each one of His disciples was the temple of the Holy Spirit, and each temple, He had to dig deep and place within each of them spiritual foundations that would endure, while working on their character. Using His same methods we must do likewise with our team of leaders because they will help us develop the vision.

CONSIDER THAT EACH CAN SHEPHERD TWELVE

"Then Jesus went about all the cities and villages, teaching in their synagogues, preaching the gospel of the kingdom, and healing every sickness among the people. But when he saw the multitudes, he was moved with compassion for them, because they were weary and scattered, like sheep having no shepherd. Then he said to His disciples, 'The harvest truly is plentiful, but the laborers are few. Therefore pray the Lord of the harvest to send out laborers into his harvest." (Matthew 9:35-38)

The Lord knew the great responsibility He had in meeting the needs of the multitudes, and He did this by calling upon His Twelve, whom He chose to solve the basic problems of shepherding the people.

In my own experience, I can say that 12 is the number of people over whom a direct, genuine, and effective pastorate can be exerted. When I have shared this principle with the pastors of other nations, they are surprised, because although we have a large church, we also have a small church.

The large church of course, being the entire congregation and the small church is made up of the groups of twelve.

The Twelve facilitate interpersonal relationships, i.e., the direct care of the disciple. If Jesus only shepherded twelve, why would we feel enabled to shepherd many more? When the congregation is too large, the people hardly have any access to the pastor. This privilege is reserved for the deacons, the Sunday school teachers and possibly one other leader, but with the principle of Twelve, everyone is shepherded.

EVERYONE MUST BE MINISTERED TO, IN ORDER TO MINISTER TO OTHERS

Someone shared the following observation with me about geese: Science has discovered why geese, especially in winter, fly south in a "V" formation. Observation has revealed that when each bird flaps its wings, it creates a vacuum for its partner behind it. By flying in a "V" formation, the flock covers at least 71 percent more distance than they could cover if they fly individually. Each time a goose abandons the formation, it feels the pressure of flying alone and quickly returns to the formation to take advantage of the power of the lift of the bird in front of it. When the lead goose gets tired, it rotates in the "V" and another takes the lead. The geese in the vanguard get feedback, in the form of quacking, from the geese behind them to keep up the speed.

Finally, if a goose leaves the formation because it is sick or has been wounded, two of its partners leave and follow him to help and protect him, staying with him until he can fly again or until he dies. They take off again by themselves or in another formation to catch up with their group.

Jesus had a continuous relationship with His Twelve, and in this type of relationship it was easy to minister often. In an intimate setting of this type of ministry, problems that the disciple has can be easily detected and uncovered so that they can be taken care of. Continuous ministry helps the leader to know his Twelve in an individual and personal way. The minister of the inner healing, deliverance, and the breaking of bondage, gives authority to the disciples to be able to help others, because one who has never been ministered to could never minister to others. This kind of ministry demands a supernatural pastorate because it becomes necessary to rely on the gifts of the Holy Spirit.

When you are ministered to, you receive the anointing to minister to others. I have noticed in different places where I hold seminars, pastors do not have anyone to minister to them. If they belong to a denomination or council, they have an annual meeting specifically for administrative and financial issues, not for their own personal and spiritual needs. When a ministry is developed through the Twelve, the group enjoys continuous personal ministry.

When a person goes through deliverance and inner healing, his life becomes a glass through which the Holy Spirit is poured, turning him into a channel of blessing for others. The great problem of many denominations is that their people have filled themselves with theology and have given biblical arguments to convince people that it is not necessary for them to go through deliverance; they believe that it is enough only to accept Jesus. Was it a genuine conversion? Was true repentance experienced? Many have not been delivered from their past ties because their conversion was superficial and they have not yet abandoned their sinful habits. They are people who have never been broken down nor have surrendered before the Lord. It is in this time of ministry, where one is confronted face-to-face with sin until brokenness comes, which signals genuine repentance.

For those who don't believe in deliverance, and therefore don't admit that it is necessary, I respect their position, but the model of Twelve is not going to work for them. The model is viable and effective when it is implemented in its totality and a requirement of the model is that every person goes through deliverance. When we had just started in the ministry, my wife and I used to minister in all the encounters. But now this task is in the hands of the people, that we have formed, and we fully trust them knowing that they have already gone through the same process. When the chains that existed in their lives were broken. They were left with the capacity to experience the Divine anointing that operates in the spiritual realm.

WHOEVER BEARS THE FRUIT RECEIVES THE RECOGNITION

"Therefore by their fruits you shall know them."
(Matthew 7:20)

Your Twelve must be fruitful disciples. As I explained in another chapter, the selection of Twelve cannot be made out of sympathy because it will not give results. That is risky. The Bible affirms that by their fruits you will know them. And we choose those who show diligence in the evangelistic process and are therefore fruitful. A fruitful person is one who has goals and makes an effort to achieve them. He sees in every new person a potential disciple and cares for him until he reaches maturity and strength in his Christian life.

CONSIDER THAT ALL ARE SOUL WINNERS

The Twelve must know, without a shadow of a doubt, that the main responsibility of every believer is evangelistic work. They have to know how to look for souls, create strategies to share the message of salvation, and be knowledgeable on how to minister.

When starting to develop the model, we allowed most of the leaders to select their Twelve from among members of the congregation. They chose people who already had a certain level of development and maturity in their Christian life. But, soon the source of candidates was depleted, hence the reason for implementing the evangelistic process of the church as priority.

Furthermore, we have the "prayer of three" which has an evangelistic objective, and is applied in the selection of the Twelve. Each believer is a winner of souls and this important principle must be in every pastor and leader's mind, to aspire to develop the model. There are many ways to win souls. For example, my Twelve in the men's net are using a strategy to visit businesses and develop seminars for businessmen, dealing with issues related to business administration, human resources, et cetera. Others are visiting schools and universities giving presentations about issues like AIDS, drug addiction and alcoholism, among other contemporary topics with the purpose of bringing the salvation message to them and encouraging them to join our cells.

The women under my wife's direction, have used the strategy of Miraculous Fishing, and have assembled up to 20,000 women in the city's coliseum, with more than 3,000 conversions in a single meeting. Each Saturday the youth are witnesses and workers in the meetings in which 600 to 1,000 new youth, convert to Christ. Each Sunday, in the congregational meetings, we see more than 800 converts, These phenomenal results occur because the people are committed to evangelistic work, and we are aware that we are primarily winners of souls. Our leaders are going out of the churches and looking for candidates to receive the gospel message.

REPRODUCTION BY HOMOGENEOUS CELL GROUPS IS IMPORTANT

We have dealt with this subject in the previous chapter and noted that the primary purpose of these groups is establishing strong relationship ties. The groups hasten the spiritual adjustment, of the new believer. Youth look for other couples with whom they can fellowship and share their experiences. The same is true with the women, men and even the children.

Man is an extremely social being. Consequently, homogeneous cell groups have characteristics that contribute to satisfying the social needs of each person. With this feature, the group's development and edification are provided through the outlet of each individual. When we wanted to implement the cells by geographical zones, results were poor, the growth was slow, and there were conflicting situations among the leaders. Before, each leader wanted to support the new believer in his zone, but now that homogeneous groups are not limited by geographic zones, the Twelve take care of their Twelve no matter where they live.

CONSIDER THE TWELVE AS YOUR ASSISTANTS

The Twelve carry on the extension of our ministry and they assist us in all its operations. At one time prior to implementing the vision of the Twelve, we had in place a co-pastor in the church.

When we went to Korea in 1990 we left him in charge, and when we returned we were surprised that, having tasted position of authority, he wanted to remain in it. We were forced to remove him, and the Lord showed us that He had a better strategy for us, the model of Twelve.

These Twelve are our close friends and assist us in everything. Interestingly, because of the murder attempt on my life, and having had to leave the country, they selected the person who would replace me. Each leader knows the vision and commits to its objectives. The pastor doesn't have to worry about someone removing the chair from under him, since this vision, by nature, requires teamwork in order to flourish. There are no personal motives, only mutual respect and consecration to the cell vision. My team of twelve has the authority to replace me whenever it becomes necessary. The same is true for the other levels of Twelve. If the leader has to be absent for any reason, one of the Twelve can temporarily take his place. The model is most efficient working this way.

FORMING AN ANNEX GROUP

The reason for the annex group is to have a team of twelve persons being trained alongside your principle Twelve. They are not substitutes, but will be ready to replace a person from the basic group of Twelve, that for any reason would have to leave. The annexed twelve contribute efficiently to the development of the vision, because they carry out the same duties as the principals and have the same responsibilities. When your team of disciples grows and multiplication begins in the church, annex groups help the vision extend without breaking its composition. Every leader-in-training must have the ability to train other leaders. They must become skilled in the work of preparation, formation and development of cell leaders. In that sense the Lord took us a step forward, not only to train the Twelve whom we call principals, but also to raise an alternate group, motivating others to participate in this powerful vision.

This annex group, generally, in made up of those who reproduce the most in their cells, once the principal team is already formed. Experience teaches that the annex group generates the greatest part of cellular growth. When you form your annex team, you must take care in choosing them from within your own ministry, because this is not about reassigning people randomly from one group to another, but it's about emulating the people as Israel did, not shifting unpredictably from one tribe to another.

FROM THE ANNEX GROUP TO THE PRINCIPAL GROUP

Someone from the annex group can aspire to join the principal group. As in professional sports, those on the bench wait for a change in the team's composition so that they may participate in the game.

There are many reasons for a member of the principal team to be absent; a job transfer out of the city, wanting to join another ministry, (in this case one would make the change with the approval of his principal leader), or the opening of a cell group in another city where he is chosen to lead it. Disciplinary actions for immoral problems may occur too. When someone has to be disciplined for some justifiable cause, that person leaves for a season and is replaced by one from the annex group. One other reason could be for lack of fruitfulness in a cell member's performance.

THE ANNEX GROUP:
TO DISCOVER TALENTS AND GIFTS

One outstanding advantage of the annex teams is that they allow for the discovery of one's talents and gifts. It is also a challenge for the leader, since through this group he can transform new believers who have potential for leadership. In addition, all who form the annex are constantly in touch with the vision, and as a result, little is needed to teach them the overall operation of the cell vision.

Those who have gained the trust of their leader and work alongside him climb high in this vision. The cell structure allows for continuous motivation so that growth is not retarded, and an important part of this motivation is associated with the annex team.

For example, my wife implemented a strategy that gave great results. First, she formed her principal Twelve. To each one she assigned one from the annex team, to motivate their spiritual growth, with the goal of elevating them to the principal group's spiritual level within a period of 3 months. The spiritual development achieved by both the principal group and the annex group was exceptional. I feel certain that these same guidelines will help you reach success in its application.

Chapter Twelve

THE TWELVE FACING
THE NEW MILLENNIUM

"A good vision will positively influence new generations."
C.C.D.

The church of Jesus Christ is experiencing one of the most extraordinary revivals of all ages. Day after day, the number of souls thirsty for hope of restoration and salvation for their lives accelerates. This means that the harvest, God has prepared for these final days is immense and we must be prepared.

Now more than ever, the fulfillment of the Great Commission is imminent. But this means not only winning souls for Christ, but discipling them so that they are able to win others.

"Go therefore and make disciples of all nations, baptizing them in the name of the Father and the Son and of the Holy Spirit, teaching them to observe all things that I have commanded you..." (Matthew 28:19-20a)

The teaching that will be given to each new believer must also train them for leadership to allow them to operate with spiritual authority and full knowledge of the Word when they go out into the entire world.

THE PRESENT AND FUTURE PANORAMA

We must be aware of the state of the world we live in. It is being shaken by needs that affect all humanity and we are witnessing a Dante-like spectacle characterized by violence, natural disasters, wars, corruption, and other scourges that make us realize how sick our society is. Most of these acts correspond to signs that the Bible describes as the gateway to the end times.

This state of anxiety and worry causes man to see only a hopeless future. However, we still have time to reveal the encouragement of the Good News to those who doubt a better future. It is the church of Christ who posses the message of peace and freedom, and declaring it requires people who are not only born again, but have full knowledge of the truth and are qualified to counterattack the forces of the enemy.

Entering the twenty-first century, the church cannot ignore the reality of the panorama that besieges us. In our case, for example, we are aware of the state of Colombia, and cannot cover our eyes with our hands and say that the country is doing well. We are dealing with political, social and economic problems just like other countries of the world, and all because some egotists in government who, in order to achieve their selfish desires, do not care who they run over. Paul says, "...*for whatever a man sows, that he will also reap*" (Galatians 6:7). That's why today, we are reaping what our forefathers have sown. What is the alternative? The church's new generation of transformed leaders is being equipped with God's answer for peace that Colombia and the world desperately need.

THE TWELVE: THE WORLD'S NEW GENERATION

"A good man leaves an inheritance to his children's children..." (Proverbs 13:22)

God has seen the affliction of His people and has provided a way out. That is why He is raising up a peculiar generation, ready for personal sacrifice so that His path of righteousness will extend before the eyes of the world. This generation is formed of men and women grateful for what the Lord has done in their lives, and aware that the change to which the rest of humanity aspires is possible as we stand together to testify of the love of Christ, and willing to be transformed in order to be reproduced in others.

The model of Twelve is the appropriate solution for the world as we see Proverbs. This model allows for good men to leave an inheritance to the sons of their sons, because when each one shepherds Twelve, and these in turn shepherd their Twelve, they are transmitting the vision and anointing to establish tangible change in their society.

Traditional church methods that don't allow each individual to develop must be broken before forging ahead. Most churches make the pastor a one-man show, the only one with the anointing to preach, heal the sick, teach in the school of leaders, lead the youth, women, men and children. All the while, the congregation is waiting for the pastor to give them an opportunity to serve. The model of Twelve is therefore a model of opportunity for every believer. It is a system where everyone can participate, after receiving adequate training; they will be able to care for the great harvest coming to the church through revival. When this model is not operating in the church, insecurity and fear of insurrection are likely to occur and could bring division or something of a similar nature. For those people, I have this advice: Learn to trust your subordinates if you aspire to have God's anointing of multiplication for the new millennium. *"The fear of man brings a snare, but whoever trusts in the Lord shall be safe."* Proverbs 29:25

THE BEST TEAM FOR THE END TIMES

"'The glory of this latter temple shall be greater than the former,' says the Lord of hosts.' And in this place I will give peace,' says the Lord of hosts"(Haggai 2:9).

The latter glory started at Pentecost with the great release of the Holy Spirit, and with the anointed message of the apostle, confirmed with signs and wonders. Later, even the dead were raised by faith of these men of God. But, the prophetic message goes further. It extends to all of God's future posterity, today's latter day saints.

When Haggai speaks of, "The glory of this latter house," he refers to the house of God, which is not made with "walls." When Jesus said, Destroy this temple, and in three days I will raise it up" (John 2:19), the Jews related it to a building. However, He was referring to His own body, His life, implying that true temple of God is not built of walls, (or traditions), but of individuals in whom He desires to manifest His presence.

The days, in which we now live, the Lord refers to as the best wine, which is reserved for the end. That's why the people of this era have a tremendous responsibility to the Lord, perhaps unlike those of previous generations. Understanding this reality, Jesus decided to do His work with

Twelve. Jesus' disciples faithfully achieved the Lord's dream and took His message to the ends of the earth. After having trained twelve fully committed men, they were known to have turned the world upside down with the gospel.

Something peculiar that we have noticed as we do His work is that He reveals Divine strategies that make the work more effective. This makes the model of Twelve dynamic and flexible; and allows us to move according to the Holy Spirit's guidance. The Lord continuously gives us new ideas for evangelism as well. Everyday we pray, "Lord, give us more creativity, renew our minds to be able to impact people with Your message, and in that way we may fulfill the task You have entrusted us."

What we have achieved up to now has exceeded all of our expectations because God gave us the best team in the world; a committed team that does not look for its own glory, but fervently labors and serves others. This is the team required for the propagation of the gospel and to achieve the greatest harvest of souls for Christ in the new millennium.

PART III

CELLULAR VISION: TWENTY-FIRST CENTURY REVOLUTION

Chapter One

THE CELLULAR VISION

"The vision is like a great field, your life is like a seed, brokenness is a planted seed, and enthusiasm is the water that makes it germinate." C.C.D.

ANOINTING OF MULTIPLICATION

Since the beginning of creation, God established the law of Genesis, which is that everything must reproduce or multiply after its own kind, and without this, it would be impossible to maintain the quality of each generation that comprised such creation. God multiplies the small and transforms it to something great.

"Then God said, 'Let the earth bring forth, the herb that yields seed, and the fruit tree that yields fruit according to its kind, whose seed is in itself, on earth;' and it was so" (Genesis 1:11).

Everything God created had as a fundamental component, the seed. To talk about seed is to speak of multiplication and reproduction of posterity.

"And God blessed them, saying, 'Be fruitful and multiply, and fill the water in the seas, and let the birds multiply on the earth" (Genesis 1:22).

Before God created man He prepared the home where he would dwell. The trees and plants had seeds. What would have happened if vegetation were created without seeds? The food would have been enough for the first generation only. It is amazing to see how modern technology has managed to grow a great variety of seedless fruits artificially, but they are only good for a moment because without seeds there is no means for them to reproduce.

The fish of the sea, the birds of the air, the beasts of the field, and all other life that God created, carry the reproduction blueprint of life. When God created man, He placed the anointing of multiplication inside him, *"Then God blessed them, and God said to them, 'Be fruitful, and multiply; fill the earth and subdue it; have dominion over the fish of the sea, over the birds of the air, and over every living thing that moves on the earth'"* (Genesis 1:28).

AND GOD BLESSED THEM

Although Adam spent a long time alone enjoying the majestic paradise around him, the full blessing wasn't released over his life until his mate arrived. The Lord could have blessed only Adam, but His plan was always about the family. The same is true with the cellular vision. It's a vision of teamwork, where the husband and wife, in agreement, work for the cell's multiplication. The husband must involve his wife since the call is for both of them. God has impressed in both our hearts that He is going to reinstate the priestly anointing at the family level, where the weight of the ministry will no longer be carried by one person, but will be distributed over whole families. That's why the man must know how to involve the woman, and the couple must know how to involve their children, so that all are an active part of the ministry. God said that by the end of time there would come a special anointing for the restoration of the family ministry, through which He will *"...turn the heart of the fathers to the children, and the heart of the children to their fathers"* (Malachi 4:6). When the family understands its responsibility to God's work, the ministry develops much faster. Even though Adam was created first, and then Eve, the full blessing did not come until God joined them as a couple.

During the first years of my ministry most of the workload was my responsibility, since my wife thought that her ministry was to care for the family. My heart's desire was that she would take a more active role in the ministry even though I continued to count on her support at home. A short time before the start of the International Charismatic Mission, God told me, *"I will awaken your wife's spirit."* After that word, I saw powerful and tangible enthusiasm in her. Since that time my wife has become 50 percent of the ministry, and acquired zeal as intense as mine. This same enthusiasm was being transmitted to the whole family. My daughters saw how the two of us were committed to the work of God, and this produced a burning desire in them. What we have experienced in our church is that when the husband and wife commit, God brings a powerful protection over the family, much greater that when the woman stays home to care for the children. The pressures that youth experience in the world are so strong that much more than maternal help is needed, and this is the fruit of a strong husband and wife ministry.

I can say through personal experience that this is a family vision, because the vision is applied in such a way that my four daughters are involved. Each one of them forms part of the group of her preceding sister. So, Lorena is part of

Johanna's Twelve, Manuela is part of Lorena's Twelve, and Sarah is part of Manuela's Twelve. We all participate in the Vision.

BE FRUITFUL

"By this My Father is glorified, that you bear much fruit..." (John 15:8).

God's blessings are reflected in fruitfulness. Every believer must become fruitful so that he can multiply. This is the Lord's established plan throughout the Bible. Fruitfulness depends on a life of sanctity. It is what God demands from each one of His children. Sanctification is the seed of God's character in our lives, given to us from the moment of creation. When God breathed the breath of life in a man, he became a living soul, acquiring the image and likeness of the triune God. God wanted His likeness reproduced in man, so it could be reproduced in all his descendants. Sanctification is a consequence of the presence of God's Spirit in the life of each believer. The Lord said, *"Be holy, for I am holy... holiness, without which no one will see the Lord."* (1Peter 1: 16, Hebrews 12:14). Sanctification must be our fruit.

The starting point for every ministry should be sanctification. If a leader experiences numerical growth, and sees that everyday more people are added to his ministry, this does not necessarily mean that God is involved. Growth without sanctification is a great distraction brought by the enemy to lead many to destruction. Growth with sanctification is God's strategy to allow many to enter through the doors of salvation. The correct spiritual order is as follows: The blessing is imparted to the couple and from a proper relationship comes fruitfulness. It is reflected in multiplication that is then conducive to authority.

The first couple centered all of their attention on procreation or multiplication, and discarded fruitfulness, or sanctity of life. As a result, people multiplied and filled the earth, but because they neglected the seed of sanctity that God placed in them, evil entered and contaminated the entire human race. That's why God later repented in his heart that He made man. He planned to destroy from the face of the earth everything He had created, but Noah found grace in God's sight. Because of Noah, God preserved mankind (Genesis 6:8). God sent the universal flood, and all creation was razed, but He preserved Noah and his family whom He blessed, telling them, *"Be fruitful and multiply, and fill the earth. And the fear of you and the dread of you shall be on every beast of the earth, and on every bird of the air, on all that move on the earth, and on all the fish of the sea. They are given into your hand"* Genesis 9:1-2).

God gave yet another opportunity to mankind, by erasing the past. The same blessings that He had declared over Adam and Eve were transferred to Noah and his family, leaving a light of hope for humanity.

I WILL BLESS YOU

"I will make you a great nation; I will bless you, and make your name great; and you shall be a blessing"
(Genesis 12:12).

God made Abraham this promise, not when he and his family were many, but when they were few. The promise didn't mean that it was going to be fulfilled the next day. It was conditioned on his obedience to God's Word. God said, *"I will make you a great nation."* This promise is accompanied by another promise, *"I will bless you."* The word bless means everything is going to be very good for him, namely, good health, mental tranquility, emotional stability, prosperity, family harmony and spiritual development.

This blessing takes one to a place of preeminence, which means that God will exalt your name, putting you in a place of authority. We observe that God's blessings are increasing, taking His children from glory to glory.

First comes the promise, then blessings and later God exalts the individual and he becomes a blessing to families, cities and nations. God decided to make a covenant with a man who lived in a pagan land with an idolatrous family, because He saw in him the light of hope to bless the families of the earth. *"And I will make My covenant between Me and you, and will multiply you exceedingly"* (Genesis 17:2). But God had to isolate him in order to work on his temperament and character. Abraham was obedient in everything; he believed the Lord and it was counted, as righteousness and he became known as a friend of God.

GETTING TO KNOW GOD AS FATHER

After 24 years of unfruitful waiting for the miracle of his promised son, God reveals to Abraham once again, *I am the Almighty God."* In the Hebrew language, *El shaddai,* means Almighty. *Shad* means chest, referring to God's maternal chest. With this revelation, God fills an emotional emptiness present in the life of the patriarch who, although 99 years old, kept latent the emotional experience of his childhood. God had to reveal that He would never fail him, suggesting that though his human father would have failed him, his Father God would not. And although his natural mother did not fully provide for his emotional needs, God manifested Himself as the one who nourishes or supplies every need that Abraham would have. After supplying his needs, He declares to him, *"Walk before me, and be perfect."*

If Abraham's heart had not been healed it would have been practically impossible for him to walk before God and be perfect. Later, God made a covenant with the patriarch. *"And I will establish My covenant between Me and you and your descendents after you."* The covenant God made with Abraham is an example for each of us: God wants to first heal our hearts so that we can then live before Him in perfection, thus establishing His covenant in us.

YOU WILL BE THE FATHER OF MULTITUDES

Once again, the process is repeated: a life of sanctity (perfection), and afterwards multiplication of one's seed. God gave us a great example through Abraham's life because He chose a husband and wife without hope of reproduction and renewed and transformed them into parents of multitudes. The only thing Abraham had to do for the miracle was to believe God. In the same way, the Lord can take a completely sterile ministry and transform it into a fruitful and reproductive one regardless of how many years it has been sterile. That's why it is important for each person to live in the dimension of faith, since without faith it is impossible to please God.

Abraham never weakened in his circumstances, even though, humanly speaking, everything was against him. But he grew strong in faith, each night he would look at the stars and could see in each of them, faces of those who would form descendants. In faith, he always thanked God for having made him a father of many nations. When everything looked hopeless for the patriarch's descendants, God said, *yes,* and Sarah conceived and bore a child. She was 99 years old, but Jacob begat the 12 patriarchs who later formed the 12 tribes of Israel. Soon, they were as numerous as the stars in the heavens and the sands of the sea.

These same principles apply to us today. If we believe God, He will give us the same ability to reproduce. Just as Abraham believed God, we too should believe, since He desires that we conquer everything in the realm of faith. We can dream and call those things that are not as though they are, calling multitudes into God's kingdom and our ministries.

Chapter Two

CELLULAR VISION:
THE LATTER REVIVAL

"Everything exists through our words. What we say determines what we will be, preparing a path of either life or death. May our words be the fruit of a life of righteousness."
C.C.D.

On the day of Pentecost, 120 people in the Upper Room represented the fullness of authority for launching the most powerful and historic event to impact the church that is still being experienced today. The assembly was complete. There were ten representatives of the twelve tribes that even included, the replacement for Judas' position that was filled by Matthias, so that the fullness of apostolic authority was well represented by the twelve groups of ten. Prior to this great revival they prayed, waiting for what God had promised: His Spirit and power. The impact was enormous because the Spirit and His power would remain with the church thereafter.

A pastor friend of mine told me about the Jewish concept of cells. He said that according to the Jews, for a cell to have authority it should have no less than 10 people.

That's why in the Upper Room there were 120 present who were representatives of the Twelve tribes of Israel. As a result of the visitation, an anointing of authority and power came over the lives of each disciple present and their messages began to be supported by a glorious and continual presence of the Holy Spirit. The first message Peter preached resulted in 3,000 new converts and in the second message an additional 5,000 were added. What did the early church do to shepherd more than 8,000 people in a personal and intimate way?

The new converts had to be cared for otherwise their spiritual development would be reduced to a simple form of encouragement. But notice that in the early church all the needs of each person were provided through a cellular infrastructure.

They met everyday at the temples and in the houses and did not cease to preach about Jesus Christ.

A month before staring the church that my wife and I lead today, God revealed Himself to me in an extraordinary way while vacationing with my family at a Colombian beach. In a message that lasted almost forty-five minutes, God told me, *"Dream of a very large church, because dreams are the language of My Spirit. The church that you will shepherd will be as numerous as the stars in the sky, and the sands of the sea; so numerous that they will be countless."* Guided by this wonderful manifestation we started the ministry with eight people gathered in our living room. God's blessings always start from the least to the greater, and are like the light of dawn that gradually increases until the day has fully arrived. A family impacted by the gospel becomes a powerful influence to motivate other families.

THE SUCCESS OF THE CHURCH IS IN THE CELLS

I am convinced that the success of the Christian church in the world depends on the way it uses the cellular vision and develops it. I also believe that the challenges of growth are so enormous that only through the development of a cellular system, the church will be able to completely disciple and prepare the people who will take the gospel to the whole world. Our goal is to reach the nations, and for that to happen it is first necessary to establish the work in the homes. Conducing a home cell meeting should be similar to taking the Old Testament shadow and type of the Ark of the Covenant, which housed the presence of the Lord and having it rest in the homes. It will radiate the light of the gospel to the whole neighborhood. By being faithful in the least, in this case a cell, the Lord will take us to much greater things.

HANDING THE MINISTRY OVER TO THE HOLY SPIRIT

When the Christian church began the Lord established it on the foundation of His Word, but before leaving this world, He handed all the church's responsibility over the Holy Spirit. When I allude to the Holy Spirit I am specifically referring to the Third Person of the Trinity. When Jesus was on earth people could see, touch and feel Him, but He told His disciples prior to departing, *"Nevertheless I tell you the truth. It is to your advantage that I go away; for if I do not go away, the Helper will not come to you; but if I depart, I will send Him unto you"* (John 16:7). Since that time, God's Spirit has had complete freedom to develop our church using the same power that flowed through the life of Jesus. Initially we tried pretending to be guided by God's Spirit and the results were poor. Then we wisely handed control over the Holy Spirit and the cell growth quickly bore fruit.

A PASTORAL VISION FROM PERSON-TO-PERSON

The traditional concept of a church is a brick and mortar building. But Jesus developed his ministry through contact with people without the limitation of church structures. Every believer must acquire basic knowledge of his Christian faith in his cell because at the very least a believer must aspire to share his faith with others, since the salvation of souls fundamentally depends on this. As St. Peter said, *"...be ready always to give an answer to every man that asks you a reason for the hope that is in you..."* (1 Peter 3:15). Every church, through the cell system, gets involved as soul winners. Even the most simple believer can gather his family who otherwise might never go to church, and through the leader of his cell, everyone can be touched by God's word. The challenge of the pastor is to get each member of his community to unite in commitment so that they can achieve the purpose for which God prepared them. Italian economist and sociologist, Vilfredo Pareto, has a formula which states that 20 percent of any business or community does the work of the remaining 80 percent. That's why we find very capable people within our churches, which prefer not to get involved, yet receive the benefits of those who do the work of the mission. But each pastor, with God's wisdom, must see to the involvement of all the members of his community.

In our ministry experience, where we have integrated a high percentage of members into our vision, it has demanded such a commitment of work from each member that there is no time for laziness or murmuring. Each one keeps busy achieving his objectives. Pastoral workload is made much lighter when the weight of the church is not centered on one single person. When the pastor involves the entire church, the results are much more successful.

SMALL GROUPS STRENGTHEN THE CHURCH

Cells are: *Small groups formed by people who meet at least once a week to develop integral growth centered on the Word of God*. Since the beginning of the early church, the growth of congregations has been the result of cells; *then the word of God spread, and the number of the disciples multiplied greatly in Jerusalem..."* (Acts 6:7).

Inside a weekly cell, instruction for the new believers is administered and at the same time members of the group are being prepared for the time when the cell multiplies.

Cells are a wonderful tool to allow its members to achieve spiritual growth in relation to God and knowledge of His word, *"But may the God of all grace, who called us to His eternal glory by Christ Jesus, after you have suffered a while, perfect, establish, strengthen and settle you"* (1 Peter 5:10). A cell has a broad effect both over personal edification of the believer and in multiplication of the mother church. This is mainly due to the fact that the process of *spiritual* cell growth is similar to the process of *biological* cell growth. In biology, the cell is the smallest unit of life and has the ability to multiply. Every cell feeds, grows and reproduces into another that has its own functions and similar characteristics to the cell from which it came.

The cell is a morphologic and physiological unit of living tissue made up of a *nucleus, centrosome, cytoplasm* and *chromosomes*. Each one of these elements participates in the cellular multiplication process. In this process, the centrosome divides and the chromosomes augment and look for a new position, which is given when the nucleus splits. Nuclei are then formed again with their respective chromosomes. In this way, each cell lives through its multiplication stage and growth is constant.

Transferring the biological concept to a spiritual point of view, there are large similarities that guide the basics of growth in the church. The *spiritual cell* makes up the smallest unit of life in the church. It is a miniature church, receiving nourishment from the Word of God, and then grows and multiplies. Each spiritual cell is made up of a host, leader, assistant and the participants.

SUCCESSFUL CELLS

A successful cell is one that has prepared twelve leaders ready to be sent. The level of success of each cell is represented by the success of each one of the leaders prepared to lead it. This group, which starts with an average of six attendees, forms for multiplication. One successful strategy used to achieve growth is the "empty chair." Leave an empty chair in each meeting and pray to the Lord for a new person to occupy it. All attendees commit to interceding for that person and to invite new people to the meeting. When attendance of 12 people is reached, the leader should start considering multiplication of a cell. Even though in the biological field it is cellular division, we prefer to use the term "multiplication." The purpose of the cell vision is the multiplication of the church.

REQUIREMENTS OF A SUCCESSFUL CELL:
- Sanctity within the cell.
- The leader must know the vision and how to convey it.
- The host must be committed to the vision, not only to know about it, but he must be developing it.
- Motivate the people to get involved in the vision (invite them to join and prepare in the School of Leaders).
- From the beginning the objective of the cell must be known: form disciples who can then form others.

TERMINOLOGY

Duplicate: *To make double (multiply by two), to make an exact copy or copies. To make, do, or cause to happen again. To form identification cells.*

Duplication occurs when in *twelve months* a cell becomes 2 accordingly, in *twenty-four months* you have 4 cells, *in thirty-six months*, 8 cells, in *forty-eight months*, 16 cells, in *sixty months*, 32 cells and in *seventy-two months* you ca achieve 64 cells.

CELLULAR DUPLICATION TABLE

Number of cells	1	2	4	8	16	32	64
Programmed time		3	6	9	12	18	24
Ideal time	12	24	36	48	60	72	

(Time is in months)

Number: Corresponds to the number of cells.

Programmed time: Theoretical frequencies of duplication measured in months.

Ideal time: Real frequencies of duplication measured in months.

CELLULAR DUPLICATION GRAPH

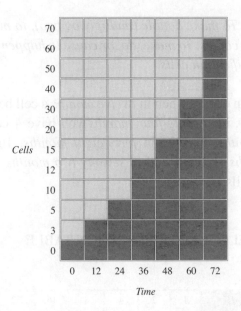

Time

Multiplication: Multi = many. To considerably augment the number of cells, taking into account that a disciple has received training to lead during nine months.

This means that in *twelve months*, the leader has managed to reproduce 12 cells, in *twenty-four months* he has reached 144 cells, in *thirty-six months* he has received 1,728 cells, in *forty-eight months* he has multiplied up to 20,736 cells. In *sixty months*, if he faithfully follows the scheme, he should achieve 248,832 cells, and in *seventy-two months* it is possible to reach the extraordinary number of 2,485,984 cells.

Cells	1	12	144	1.728	20.736	248.832	2´485.984
Ideal time		12	24	36	48	60	72

(Time in Months)

CELLULAR MULTIPLICATION GRAPH

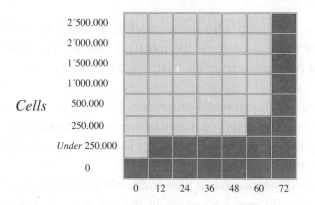

The following table shows difference between number of cells reproduced by the *duplication* method and the multiplication method, during the same period of time *(in months):*

Actual Time	2	2	24	36	48	60	72
Difference	0	10	140	1.720	20.720	248.800	2´485.912

(Difference, multiplication vs. duplication)

COMPARATIVE GRAPHIC: DUPLICATION VS. MULTIPLICATION

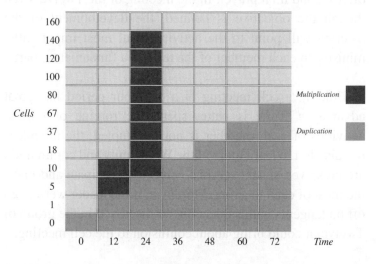

CELLS, THE SOURCE OF THE TWELVE

From the group who meets weekly, a selection can be made of those who show the most promise of fruitfulness and can be nominated to the basic team of leaders.

There are fundamental differences between the Cell and the Twelve. The cell is open to whoever wishes to attend and the meeting of the Twelve is only for its members of the team of workers.

The cell meeting has a time limit, while the meetings of the Twelve do not. Instruction in the cell level is directed towards the edification of the believer, whereas in the meeting of the Twelve, the instruction is more directed towards leadership.

Furthermore, the Twelve can be a product of the cell, but they are made up of a team of workers. In the cell, the activities accomplished in the short time period of the meeting are clearly defined: the welcome, initial prayer, brief testimonies, praise, teachings, prayer for individual needs, offering and final prayer. In the meeting of the Twelve, even though the objective is defined, the development of the meeting will point to the activities, but most importantly, ministry to each member of the team is a fundamental part.

Holding a cell meeting in a one-hour period has great advantages. Time is better spent, the routine or normal activities of each member is not interrupted, the attendees remain alert to learn more of the Word, unity and communion are preserved since everyone wants to participate and make the most of each meeting. Moreover, if the leader were to go off on tangents with subject matter discussed in the group of Twelve, it could bring about confusion to the cell meeting.

Every leader must acknowledge that the Bible is our manual and that prayer unifies us. They therefore cannot be missing from the meetings furthermore, the leader must avoid entertaining negative comments. In the cell, edification is mutual, that's why it must be imparted with love because love demonstrates acceptance and forgiveness and love looks out for everyone's best interests. I am sure this is God's strategy for the next millennium. The church that aspires to conquer the world for Christ, must do its work based on the cell vision. The church must become a church without walls because walls limit God's work. Each house must be a small temple where the Holy Spirit is poured out as it occurred in the Book of Acts on the day of Pentecost.

Chapter Three

A VISION FULL OF
SPIRITUAL AUTHORITY

*"Become friends with the Holy Spirit and He will give
you His anointing, love the model of Twelve and you will
have direction, work with the cells and you will have
multiplication."* C.C.D.

The spiritual authority the Lord establishes with the cell
vision structure is what allows for its success. Paul' request
in prayer from the Father of Glory was that He, *"...may give
to you the spirit of wisdom and revelation in the knowledge
of Him"* (Ephesians 1:17). Furthermore, Solomon said,
"...wisdom brings success" (Ephesians 10:10). There are
times when as leaders we have to make delicate and difficult
decisions. Wisdom is necessary for us to lead and He gives
us an anointing for guidance every step of the way. The
goal we had set for 1995 was to finish the year establishing
200 churches in Bogotá, a very broad and challenging goal
that we thought was the vision the Lord wanted for us. We
were six months into the training of the pastors for our new
churches, when an opportunity came for me to travel to
Seoul, Korea to visit Dr. Cho's ministry at Yoido Full Gospel
Church. The experience during this visit was forever in my
memory.

While attending one of Pastor Cho's Sunday morning
church services, I remained standing because there were no
available seats. Looking towards the platform I saw a vision,

247

as it were. God showed me Pastor Cho wearing an athletic outfit holding a torch and approaching me to hand it to me as if to say, *"Now it's your turn to continue."* It was then that I heard the voice of the Spirit say, *"Son, I gave you a vision similar to this man's vision, a large church with many cells, and you have tried to introduce another vision within Mine, that is divisive."* I began to realize that the vision I was given by the Lord was not identical to Dr. Cho's, although it was similar. I was trying to inject another man's vision into His vision. Although I thought I was doing the right thing, the Lord prompted me that that was not what He had for me at the time. Humanly speaking, it sounds extraordinary to open 200 new churches in one year, but in Divine wisdom the important objective should always be His will. Paul said, *"One thing only I do."* God's wisdom consists of working on one single thing, the vision He gives us. Pitifully, many of us make the same mistake, and wanting to do more, we do less. I repented before the Lord and I promised I would return to the original vision.

When I returned to Bogotá, I assembled my leaders and told them: *"Brothers, I am embarrassed to say I was wrong, we are not opening 200 new churches. When we make a mistake, we have to accept it, ask for forgiveness, and change our attitude."* I left the leadership with a new challenge, to multiply our cells during the rest of the year. Thank the Lord things went even better than what we had imagined. We grew from 1,200 cells to 4,000 cells in only six months. Although we diverted away from God's original vision, He received us back into His will for our lives. If we act hastily we will make errors and this will be reflected in a stagnant ministry.

That's why we should always ask the Lord for the necessary wisdom to make the right decisions.

AUTHORITY IMPLIES
REVELATION KNOWLEDGE

Wisdom is necessary to lead each aspect of our life and ministry, but revelation allows us to understand the plans God has for that ministry. While wisdom leads us, revelation informs us, and it tells us what to do in different situations. God has all knowledge and He was pleased to fully deposit it into our lives. *"That the God of our Lord Jesus Christ, the Father of glory, may give to you the spirit of wisdom and revelation in the knowledge of Him"* (Ephesians 1:17).

On one occasion I assembled a group of leaders and the Spirit started showing me different sins that some of them had committed. When these hidden things came to light by the word of knowledge, the 130 men assembled there, fell to their knees asking for forgiveness from the Lord. During the next week, they consecrated themselves with fasting, bringing full sanctification to that branch of the ministry. Similarly, we see what happened with Peter when Anaias and his wife Sapphira lied to the Holy Spirit. They were exposed and both dropped dead at the apostle's feet. In the same way, sanctification reveals who has a perfect heart towards God and the vision; and who is infiltrating within the ranks to contaminate God's plans. Furthermore, the Lord showed me that person in this same meeting was the sin of Achan, (who had lied and hidden Jericho's loot). Instantly, one of the leaders present stood up confessing his sin saying that that was exactly what he had done, whereupon immediately a reverent fear fell over the whole group. After that experience, those men were never the same.

It is not necessary for human sources to interfere whenever Divine revelation is exposing sin because the Holy Spirit is in charge of revealing the thoughts and intentions of the heart.

This revelation knowledge should be continually present in the church to prevent the infiltration of any hypocrisy, thus maintaining the church's sanctity, purity and honesty. Those men who were used to living a double life were totally broken down in that meeting because their conviction of sin was too powerful to resist.

THE AUTHORITY AND CREATIVE POWER OF THE WORD

The Lord Jesus Christ said, *"But I say to you that for every idle word men may speak, they will give account of it in the Day of Judgment. For by your words you will be justified, and by your words you shall be condemned"* (Matthew 12:36-37).

The Lord always acts in harmony with His Word. Scriptures say that before creating the world the Word existed, and Jesus Christ is that Word. It also says, *"...the Word was with God, and the Word was God. He was in the beginning with God."* When God planned in His heart to create the world and man, He simply sent His Word. The Word of God when expressed is so powerful that it causes the whole army of the heavenlies to act. A single word from Him can give life and turn chaos into order. God made the universe out of nothing. In the natural realm nothingness is something that doesn't exist, but in the spiritual realm nothingness is something invisible that is brought into the visible realm through faith.

This allows us to understand the greatness of Divine sovereignty. He sent the Word and nothing became something. As is expressed in the book of Hebrews, *"By faith we understand that the worlds were framed by the word of God, so that things which are seen were not made of things which are visible"* (Hebrews 11:13). What we see here is that God created all things out of nothing. The apostle Peter said that God's promises make us partakers of the Divine nature (2 Peter 1:4). This means that, although we may not initially see any ministry fruit, we should first take hold of the desires in our heart, submit them to the Lord and cooperate with the Holy Spirit to bring them into the natural realm through faith. But it is important that each one know his objective and has the conviction that it can be achieved. When Jesus preached the people declared, *"This man speaks with authority."* When he faced the possessed demons, they had to bow on their knees because they recognized His authority. By Jesus simply commanding, *"Get out of him,"* demons trembled and shook, even begged, *"Lord, if you expel us, let us go into the pigs."* The Lord simply said, *"Go,"* and that word was all that was needed for them to obey. Sometimes we think that if we multiply our words God will listen to us even more attentively, but that is not so. The Jews are said to be short on words and in the Hebrew language their vocabulary has only 10,000 words. Compare this with the Greek language, having more than 200,000 words. The Lord doesn't want man to use many words because He is more interested in faith-filled words of truth.

The words of Jesus Christ were few but they revolutionized the whole world. God's Words divided history in two, they brought hope to anguished and desperate hearts, opened new freedom for the sick and destitute, and with them, Jesus became the only one who could provide for the needs of this world. The Lord placed the same power in our reach when He said, *"For assuredly, I say to you, whosoever says to this mountain, 'Be removed and be cast into the sea,' and does not doubt in his heart, but believes that those things he says will be done, he will have whatever he says"* (Mark 11:23).

A GREAT TEAM

Jesus Christ became the Divine expression of our Heavenly Father and His will was transmitted and revealed through this extraordinary man. While He was in this world Jesus manifested authority and power because He was aware of His Divine nature, and His Word was accompanied by the power of the Holy Spirit. This union was accompanied by the power of the Holy Spirit. This union was God's dynamite, operating in Him. Every believer should cultivate a friendship with the Spirit and the Word.

GUARDING OUR SPEECH

The Lord never spoke a complaining word. Every word spoken from His lips was edifying. Nowadays, we have societies where people have grown accustomed to using words of cursing, complaining or negativism. Curse words attract demonic powers and words of life attract God. Spoken words of faith, victory and hope immediately give angels the freedom to work on behalf of those declaring them, working in line with what has been declared. This is the power in words.

King Solomon said, *"You are snared by the words of your mouth; you are taken by the words of your mouth. So do this, my son, deliver yourself; for you have come into the hand of your friend..."* (Proverbs 6:2-3).

Man entangles himself in what he says because his words attract spiritual forces. Therefore a person can be tied to his words in blessings or curses.

EXAMPLES OF AUTHORITY

When Joshua was fighting to conquer the land of Canaan, it was getting dark in one of his fiercest battles and he knew that this would hinder defeating his enemies. He assumed an attitude of faith and raised his voice, declaring, *"Sun, stand still over Gibeon; and Moon, in the Valley of Aijalon"* (Joshua 10:12). His words were few but immediately the movement of the sun and the moon stopped and there was no light. His enemies were waiting for night to fall, but it didn't because one man understood the power of words. Joshua acted in faith and God honored him.

Solomon said, *Death and life are in the power of the tongue, and those who love it will eat its fruit* (Proverbs 18: 21). If you start to change the way you act, think and talk, and begin to see yourself as the person who God wants you to be, your life and your ministry will radically change. The enemy wants to make you look small, but you must understand that God has placed you as the head and not the tail.

Jesus characteristically acted and spoke with authority and so must you.

Observe that when a policeman stands on a main avenue and extends his hand, even the largest moving trucks must obey his authority and stop. Likewise, the Lord gave us the authority of His Word when He told His disciples, *"Most assuredly, I say to you, he who believes in me, the works that I do he will do also; and greater works than these he will do, because I go to my Father"* (John 14:12). We will see extraordinary miracles only if we believe and stand on the Word of God.

I was praying for a retired general of the age of 73 years who had been paralyzed for 8 years. I asked, *"General, do you believe God will heal you?"* He looked at me and said, *"I am so old that I can hardly believe a miracle could happen."* Like him, many people accept that sickness will take control of their bodies. But I didn't listen to his negative attitude. I talked to him about the healing promises for his life and as I explained the Scriptures, his faith increased. Then he asked me to pray for him and he repeated the prayer of faith. I then laid hands on him and told him, *"In the name of Jesus, get up and walk!"* He stood up.

His two legs looked so frail that it looked like he was going to fall down, but I told him, *"Start walking in the name of Jesus."* He started taking a few steps, and as he walked his legs became stronger.

That day, this man experienced the greatest miracle of his life and it stayed with him until the day of his death. Words of authority have power to move even the highest, most insurmountable mountain. God wants to take each of His children to the same level of authority possessed by the Lord Jesus.

BIBLICAL AUTHORITY OF THE CELLS

All aspects related to the vision have defined biblical origin. While at dinner with other pastors from Bogotá during my visit with Dr. Cho, he was explaining how the cell system had experienced remarkable growth in his church. A pastor came by and whispered in my ear, *"That cell thing might work in Korea, but it won't work here in Colombia."* But I told myself, *"I'm sure cells work in Korea, in Colombia, and in any place in the world. I know that this is the vision of God for the church in these last days."*

Although in the beginning we tried to implement the cell model in the same way as it was done in Korea, the results were not the same. This moved me to search in prayer, for a strategy that could be adapted to our setting. That's how, in 1990, God removed the veil of limitation and revealed to me the potential growth through the Twelve. Today we are committed to an eminently cellular church, which has brought spiritual maturity to thousands of families in our nation, while being the platform to develop large numbers of leaders. We know that the successful work of the early church was mainly due to their cell activities in homes. The essence of the cell system is found in the work of the early church. What took place in homes at that time is the same thing that takes place today in home cells but only when the vision is correctly applied.

Chapter Four

JESUS: CELL LEADER
BY EXCELLENCE

"Those who possess a poor self-image need to be led, those who possess a high self-image are exposed in order to be humbled, but those who possess a correct self-image will be praised." C.C.D.

JESUS MINISTERED CONTINUOUSLY IN HOMES

It was in homes where the Lord Jesus ministered to and gathered most of His followers. They were made up of publicans, prostitutes, thieves and many who were despised by Jewish society. The following text is a confirmation of this ministerial fruit in homes:

"Now it happened, as Jesus sat at the table in the house, that behold, many tax collectors and sinners came and sat down with Him and his disciples." (Matthew 9:10)

The Lord Jesus broke all sacred traditions held by the religious leaders of His day. They couldn't see how a Jew would fellowship with a Gentile, let alone go to the house of one. They held Gentiles as unclean and any fellowship with them would contaminate them. That's why they looked scornfully at many of the things Jesus did. But He wanted to teach them some truths:

He selected one whom they considered a sinner and lodged in his house. Jesus transformed him and he later became one of His apostles.

He used this situation to impart truths to a group of publicans, possibly friends of Matthew.

He demonstrated the great lesson that God's will is to reach lost souls and heal the sick because this is a display of the love and mercy of God.

LEARNING TO MINISTER FOR THE LORD

Forming a committed team requires that we have the highest spiritual credentials. This is so that those whom we disciple have the desire to emulate us. It is unlike what happens in many homes where children want to emulate their friends and not their parents, because of bad parental standards. Ministries whose members do not want to emulate their pastors exist as well.

A leader may have people following behind him every step of the way because they see something in his life that they want to emulate, and that's usually when they become disciples. The word *disciple* comes from *discipline* because individuals acquire certain spiritual disciplines that they observe in their leader, the character of Christ, for example, and they therefore want to become followers of Christ.

Leadership is established over the foundation of relationships. If we can love our fellow man it is going to be easy to form a relationship with God, and it follows that *if you cannot love your brother whom you can see, how can you love God whom you cannot see?* To minister God's heart to others we must understand that the Lord requires that each of us serve Him even before we do anything else.

THE RIGHT KIND OF SERVICE

"And which of you, having a servant plowing or tending sheep, will say to him when he has come in from the field, 'Come at once and sit down to eat'? But will he not rather say to him, 'Prepare something for my supper, and gird yourself and serve me till I have eaten and drunk, and afterward you will eat and drink?' Does he thank that servant because he did the things that were commanded him? I think not. So likewise you, when you have done all those things which you are commanded, say, 'We are unprofitable servants. We have done what was our duty to do.'" (Luke 17:7-10)

The Lord presents two aspects of the servants to Him. One has to do with the physical service to God and the other with ministering to God's heart. Many are so busy working for God's mission that they have forgotten about the *Lord of the mission*. Some think that teaching in the cells or ministering to people under their responsibility, even sacrificing time to fulfill the mission, is enough to show that they are doing a great work for the Lord.

The servant, who is plowing or tending the herd, when he returns to the house, knows that his duty is to attend to his Lord.

Generally, our work in the ministry becomes a reflection of our ministry to God's heart. If we spend time daily in His presence, our work will not be delayed or stifled because the people will see Christ's character in us.

In order for people to hear God's voice through their leader, the leader must have invested sufficient time with Him to satisfy His heart. Results will be reflected practically in all areas of his life.

IS IT A WASTE?

When an individual dedicates his life to God's service, some consider it to be a waste of time. Is it not strange that even the apostles were surprised that a common woman who was a sinner would take advantage of an opportunity to approach Jesus uninvited? Her intention was to show Him her love by taking an alabaster box full of high-priced perfume, and pouring it on the Lord's head. The attitude of this woman bothered the apostles and they became indignant saying, *"Why this waste? This perfume could have been sold for a large sum, and the money given to the poor"*
(Matthew 26:8-9).

When I began my Christian life I had to face my family's opposition since they thought that investing my time in Christianity was wasteful. On a few occasions I was recriminated for it until they chose to ignore me, maybe thinking that if I was ready to waste my life in this new belief or pursuit, they sure would not do the same. But as the years have passed my family has understood that surrendering one's life to the Lord is the best investment a human being can make. Some consider it more profitable to work in a secular business than to serve God. Others resist committing to the vision fearing it will take time away from caring for their children, and therefore do not dare take that step forward. But our ministerial experience shows us that the vision is so emotional and passionate that the whole family usually gets involved, forging powerful ties of the family unity.

The Lord was so pleased with that common woman's attitude that He immortalized her, saying that wherever the gospel would be preached the story would also be told in her memory.

To waste one's life in Christ brings the most extraordinary satisfaction. Seeing thousands of lives and families transformed by the power of God produces a joy so special, that it is difficult to find anything in this world that surpasses it. The best decision that a human being can make is to invest every day of his life serving God.

FOLLOWING THE LEADER OF LEADERS

Jesus' personality was such that He attracted multitudes. However, He knew that in some homes His presence was very important, so He prioritized these types of visits. As it happened in Jairus' case, who, amid anguish and pain over the loss of his daughter, decided to do to Jesus and entreat Him to go to his house because he needed a miracle that only the Master could perform.

During Jesus' visit to Jairus' household, the Lord said, " *Make room for the girl is not dead, but sleeping. And they ridiculed Him. But when the crowd was put outside, He went in and took her by the hand, and the girl arose. And the report of this went out into all that land"*
(Matthew 9:24-26).

So much power emanated from the Lord Jesus that He became the only hope for the world, as the prophet said; *whoever was in darkness saw great light.* And when Jesus entered a house many came to Him because they knew that He had the answer to their needs. So they made the effort not to lose an opportunity to experience a miracle in their lives or the lives of their relatives and friends. Luke narrates the case of the paralytic man who was brought to Jesus by friends, but couldn't approach Him because of the multitude. So they went up to the roof of the house, and through the roof tiles they lowered his cot into the middle of the room right in front of Jesus. When He saw their faith, Jesus told him, *"Man, your sins are forgiven you"* (Luke 5:20).

For many years I tried to picture in my mind what that moment would have been like. Jesus was so overwhelmed by people that many times He felt smothered. A few months after starting the International Charismatic Mission, our home was where the meetings took place. On a weekly basis, our home was thronged with people. Many people came in search of a miracle, or simply to worship and thank God. Although the living room had the capacity for 120 people, an average of 500 attended every meeting. The crowd overflow would be put in the garage, the bedrooms and in the garden. Also, the traffic was very impressive, to say the least.

I remember one day when I was late to a meeting that had already begun. It took me twenty minutes to reach the podium because there was not path to walk past the people. Imagine a sick man desiring prayer; generally, he would have to wait for everyone to leave so that we could pray for him. With the cell vision in place, we were able to supply the spiritual needs of many.

There was absolutely nothing that took the Lord by surprise and when the disciples were disputing about which one of them would be the greatest, the Lord asked, *"What was it you disputed among yourselves on the road?"* (Mark 9:33).
"Then He took a little child and set him in the midst of them. And when He had taken him in His arms, He said to them, 'Whoever receives one of these little children in My name receives Me; and whoever receives Me, receives not Me, but Him who sent me." (Mark 9:36-37)

There are many issues over which leaders will argue amongst themselves, but the greatest leader is he who has the strongest spirit of service. Jesus, who was the greatest expression of God's love, dwelled in His disciples' hearts and His character was being reproduced in each of them. But it was necessary that they stay in that spirit of love, not as a matter of formality, but as a specific commandment from the Lord.

PAUL, AN INSTRUMENT IN THE HANDS OF GOD

Since the beginning of Christianity many homes have been opened for preaching the gospel. Even the apostle Paul had the opportunity to form a cell at the home of a principal of Rome's synagogue, *"And he continued there a year and six months, teaching the word of God among them"* (Acts 18:11)

God touched Crispus' heart. He made the decision to serve the Lord with his entire household. This testimony spread throughout Corinth and many had the courage to surrender their lives to the Lord, testifying through water baptism. God talks to the apostle in a vision and tells him he should not be afraid because He himself would be watching for his safety. This motivated Paul to stay a year-and-a-half in that place, preaching and persuading men to worship God, not by the letter of the law, but by grace. The work that Paul had to develop must have been extensive because the moral behavior of the Corinthians was extremely liberal. Even the expression "to corinthize" became popular, referring to immorality. But God used Paul greatly on behalf of the inhabitants of this city, and that is why Paul presents them, as a letter of guarantee when he remarks, *"If I am not an apostle to others, yet doubtless I am to you. For you are the seal of my apostleship in the Lord"* (1 Corinthians 9:2).

A short time after beginning our church we felt a heavy burden in our hearts for the spiritual development of our people. My greatest concern was how to be in continuous contact with them. Because of this concern, the desire to develop discipleship activities in their homes came up. But I also understood my own limitations, thus, if I was at one place, I couldn't be in another at the same time. Even though I had many meetings to lead every week I felt others had to do the same, but that they must act with my own spirit. To be able to reproduce the vision correctly, I saw the need to equip them personally and on an ongoing basis. I understood that if there weren't ant people developed and trained for the ministry, there could be no cells. In the famous Aesop's Fables, the lesson that you can't count your eggs before they hatch has strong application in reference to cell work, i.e., if there aren't any developed people, we cannot count them. The best leaders we have are those formed since the inception of this vision.

Chapter Five

THE HOLY SPIRIT IN THE
VISION OF THE CELLS

"A Strong man controls his spirit, a wise man directs his desire, an enthusiastic man conquers nations, and a humble man transforms hearts." C.C.D.

SHAPING THE CHURCH

The participation of the Holy Spirit is always fundamental in the perfection of God's work. When God was creating the universe the Spirit moved amid the chaos, waiting for the Word of God to execute the desires of the Father's heart. The power of the Holy Spirit is indescribable and is subject to the Father's will, hence, only when God spoke did He feel complete freedom to act. The psalmist said,

"You send forth Your Spirit, they are created; and You renew the face of the earth." (Psalm 104:30)

In the same way that the Spirit had influence in the creation of man, He also takes charge in giving life to all those who are dead in their trespasses and sins. The Lord said:

"And when He has come, He will convict the world of sin, and of righteousness, and judgment." (John 16:8)

It was the Holy Spirit who convinced Thomas of his of unbelief, who then fell to his knees, exclaiming, *"My Lord and my God!"* (John 20:28). The Spirit too, used the stare of Jesus to reprove Peter after he denied Him thrice, *"So Peter went out, and wept bitterly"* (Luke 22:62).

A short time before the Lord ascended to heaven, He instructed His disciples not to leave Jerusalem until they received the promise of the Father, the Spirit of Truth. When He did come, they received power and testified about the Lord. This they did progressively, starting from their city unto the outermost parts of the earth. The Lord tried to convey to them that the Holy Spirit was active in His life during His entire earthly ministry, and, after His departure the Spirit would not manifest in one particular person, but in many who would form the church. This would demand arduous work on their part because everything would depend on the way that they disseminated this message.

KEEPING A GENUINE RELATIONSHIP WITH HIM

I cannot imagine how the development of the church could have happened without the help of the Holy Spirit. Someone dared to comment that the most ignored person of this century has been the Holy Spirit. Even though it has been 2,000 years since the glorious experience of the Pentecost in the lives of those early believers, some religious leaders refuse to surrender total control of their ministries to God's Spirit, and instead choose to displace Him from their organizations. But if we look back, we see that the whole development of the church revolved around the Holy Spirit. On the day of Pentecost the 120 disciples were filled with the Holy Spirit and God took control of their tongues. The spirit expressed through their tongues words they didn't know.

Prior to the flood, God used tongues in the Genesis account to confuse the people when they moved with an arrogant attitude and attempted to build an empire that would rise to the heavens. They declared, *"Come let us build ourselves a city, and a tower whose top is in the heavens; let us make a name for ourselves, lest we be scattered abroad over the face of the whole earth"* (Genesis 11:4). God confused their language so that they would not understand one another. This action thus hindered the profane structure those men were determined to build. In contrast, the event of Pentecost was completely different because the manifestation of tongues was the means God used for the edification of His church.

"It was the spirit who gives life; the flesh profits nothing. The words that I speak to you, they are spirit, and they are life." (John 6:63)

Immediately following Pentecost, Peter, inspired by God's Spirit, stood up and delivered his excellent dissertation that brought conviction of sin to thousands of Jews, inviting them to repentance and baptism. They then received the Holy Spirit (Acts 2:38-39). The presence of the Spirit in the apostolic ministry was such that, *"...through the hands of the apostles many signs and wonders were done among the people. And they were all with one accord in Solomon's Porch"* (Acts 5:12).

One of my prayers has been, *"Lord, allow our people to be as committed to your mission as were the believers in that early apostolic era."* As the years have passed, I have seen that our people greatly love to serve the Lord and this appears to be above economic incentives or any other kind of incentive, since their greatest honor is to have the opportunity to develop as ministers.

Fifteen years ago, pastoral work was less attractive because of my wrong concept about pasturing. But today if you ask any of our youth what their greatest wish is, their reply would be *to serve in the ministry*. We are eyewitnesses of how God transforms a whole culture. And that's what we believe has happened, that God has raised a new generation within our nation, who constitute the other face of Colombia. I know that the Holy Spirit is the only one responsible for this great spiritual awakening that we are experiencing. When our people don't care if they spend whole nights in prayer, or participate in different fasting programs, or come to church in the early hours of the morning worshiping the Lord before going about their daily activities, something has awakened! A person who visited us from Brazil and after participating in some of the regular activities of the church, made the following remark to me,

"The early church met everyday at the temple and in the homes. But this church meets everyday throughout the day, because activities are continuous in all the different ministries."

God's glory descended on the disciples' celebration of Pentecost, when all were endued with the Holy Spirit's anointing and began to change the world with the message of Christ. I am convinced that just as it happened to them, the basis for entering the cell vision and to successfully develop it is in the fullness of the Holy Spirit.

Many cell programs have failed because they have been established without the presence of the Holy Spirit and simply become men's models. Without the influence of the Holy Spirit everything we do relies on human strength and technique. Sooner or later, everything human becomes monotonous and the monotonous ends up being forgotten.

The best way to understand the cellular concept is by entering the dimension of the Spirit. It is necessary to nurture a continuous relationship with Him and be sensitive to His voice for success.

There are those pastors who have suggested to me not to emphasize the spiritual aspects because they are more interested in the method. But just as the body without the spirit is dead, the cellular vision without the Holy Spirit is a dead vision. In fact, it wouldn't be considered a vision at all.

IGNORING THE HOLY SPIRIT, DIVERTS GOD'S PURPOSE

God is looking for those who believe in Him, obey His Word, and act under the direction of the Spirit.

"If you love me, keep My commandments. And I will pray the Father, and He will give you another Helper, That He may abide with you forever; the Spirit of truth; whom the world cannot receive, because it neither sees Him nor knows Him: but you know Him, for He dwells with you and will be in you." John 14:15-17

Notice, Jesus highlights the Holy Spirit as the Spirit of truth, and ignoring Him implies denying God's purpose for our lives. My family and I have committed to develop an intimate relationship with the Holy Spirit and this requires great sensitivity to Him. I remember an experience with my wife during one of our annual conventions, which left us with a great lesson in this area. Claudia and I almost never quarrel. Our relationship has always been characterized as having harmony, unity, and mutual understanding. However, at the beginning of this important event for the church in January of 1997, we had a small difference of opinions to which I paid no attention. Because of my wife's temperament she remained sad, and I responded with silence trying to ignore her.

I tried to forget about the matter and, as if nothing happened, I began the service. Then Charles Martin, one of our guests for this event, started ministering a prophetic sound through the saxophone. Simultaneously, the Spirit gave interpretation of the prophetic melody to my wife who clearly understood each one of the sounds emitted by that anointed instrument.

The Lord told her, *"Daughter, what you experienced with your husband was allowed by Me because I wanted to give you an illustration of what is happening with My church. Just as you felt sad because your husband ignored and treated you as if you did not exist, imagine how My Spirit feels when the church ignores Him, when the days, weeks, and even months go by and My sons don't recognize Him. Just as a marriage should enjoy a proper spiritual relationship, each one of My Spirit sons must strive to maintain an excellent relationship with My Spirit because maintaining communion with one's spouse is equivalent to communion with My Spirit."*

Far from knowing what had happened to Claudia, I called her up on the stage so that she could address the almost 20,000 people gathered that day. She started to cry. Amid tears, she started to share with the audience about our disagreement. She talked about the way she felt when I had practically ignored her and talked about how God's Spirit used this situation to show her and the church about the way He feels when we ignore Him daily. Just as in the natural realm, so it is in the spiritual realm.

While she was sharing her experience, the people began to weep and felt with strong conviction the message of rebuke by the Holy Spirit. My wife and I both realized that if we give place to discord, the entire church will soon find out because we cannot have secrets with the Lord or His church.

We cannot achieve great objectives and fruitful ministries if we ignore God's Holy Spirit. It's through Him that the gifts flow, and He also gives us authority to break demonic powers that operate within families and individuals. Our task is to wins souls and make disciples, but it is not a work that can be done in the intellectual sphere of self-sufficiency. In our task, God intervenes to use us as instruments in His hands. But we are successful only when the Holy Spirit is involved in the process.

Chapter Six

THE TEN COMMANDMENTS
OF THE CELLS

"Wise men discern the times they are living in. They know when the fruit is mature, and they diligently link others to help them in the harvest so that the fruit is not lost." C.C.D.

The Divine laws rule the entire universe. The law of gravity was established since the time God commanded the earth to stay in its place. In the same was every celestial body obeys the command established by the Lord so that the sun cannot get closer or further from earth but remains where God commands it to stay. In the universe, we are all subject to the boundaries or laws pre-established by the Lord. Therefore, when we operate in them we enjoy their benefits. Just as natural laws can be violated, there are spiritual laws that man tries to willfully violate. Some even boast, *"Laws were made to be broken."* But we know that when laws are broken it is difficult to evade the consequences.

In ancient times, God gave the people of Israel the Ten Commandments that were required to guide their lives. In the same way, if we want the cell vision to develop correctly, and we want our ministry and leadership to be fruitful, certain guidelines must be considered. In our experience, certain fundamental rules should be observed for success in the cellular vision.

The following *Ten Commandments* must become a valuable support for your cell ministry:

FIRST COMMANDMENT:
LOVE THE CELLULAR VISION

Our love of what we have and what we do fights against our doubts and prepares the way for attaining success. Anyone who desires to put in action this vision and obtain the best results must completely love this vision and be ready for change in his life. The Ephesian church began with a great commitment to the Lord and an extraordinary passion for lost souls. They strove to reach the lost for Christ but as the years passed, their ministerial work became mechanical. Much work was performed but it was done without love. For that reason the Lord sent them a letter of reprimand for having left their first love (Revelation 2:4).

Where there is no love there is nothing profitable. *"And though I have the gift of prophesy, and understand all mysteries, and all knowledge and though I have all faith, so that I could remove mountains, but have not love, I am nothing. And though I bestow all my goods to feed the poor, and though I give my body to be burned, but have not love, it profits me nothing"* (1 Corinthians 13:2-3). Initially, if you take love out of the cells you've started wrong. Love your cells deeply.

When one of our pastors asked the youth ministry pastor, *"How deeply can I reach the youth and make our group grow?"* The answer he gave left him completely astonished. He replied, *"Love them!"* That's exactly what that pastor did, and in a few months he saw outstanding results. I must clarify that this type of deep love was not always present, nor was it in every leader's cell. But it has been a process where, step-by-step, each one has committed to love until it became their priority. For example, our worship minister

274

sang beautifully and her songs were very edifying, but she had only 16 cells, which was a very small number when I considered the growth rate of the church.

When I requested an explanation and she told me her main job was the vision since everyone in our church, regardless of which ministry they belonged to, must work in cells. She obliged and in the first year she went from 16 to 100 cells. Since then, her love for the cellular vision has been intense and she now has the most cells within the woman's net. This is all because she put a priority on the cells, together with demonstrating a deep love for them.

A similar situation occurred with my mother-in-law who leads the intercession ministry. Once, when I consulted her about cells, she answered, *"You know that my work consists of praying for you everyday. If you demand cells from me, who is going to intercede for your ministry?"* I explained to her that this was not something domestic or familiar, but that it was part of the vision and that we should all commit to the cells. At first, she thought I was telling her this because I wanted to transfer her to another ministry, but she later understood that it was the next step she had to take.

Overcoming all the arguments that arose in her mind, in particular, that cells were a responsibility for younger people because they have the time to do the work, she understood that age was not a factor either. Since God is not respecter of persons, she was ready to take that step of faith, and in one year she reached 100 cells. These results were possible because she put her love in the cell vision.

Age doesn't matter. My mother is 77 years old and she is involved with cells. Occupation is not a factor either. Most of the cell leaders work full time in a secular business, but they are dedicated to this vision and continue to stay motivated. The key is love.

SECOND COMMANDMENT:
DO NOT DIVERT FROM THE CELL VISION

One of the fundamental aspects of the cell vision is perseverance, i.e., being faithful to the vision, since diverting away from it can be imperceptibly easy. I have shared many experiences in previous chapters that bring to light this issue and the importance of staying focused. When the Lord spoke to me during a service at Dr. Chos's Yoido Gospel Church in Seoul, Korea, it was made clear to me that the vision given to Dr. Cho was not the same one given to me, although similar. When I explained this to my leadership they understood and were willing to go with what the Lord was directing.

THIRD COMMANDMENT:
DO NOT ALLOW THE CELL
TO BECOME UNFRUITFUL

Every cell has to be evangelistic in nature. You must go out and look for the people. When the members of the cell have weekly or monthly growth, everyone makes an effort to do their part. The Lord said, *"I have chosen you to bring forth fruit, much fruit, and that your fruit should remain."* The three stages of fruitfulness: Begin with a cell, after twelve months you should have twelve cells, and in twenty-four months you should have reached 144 cells.

Bringing for fruit (John 15:2). This is an evangelistic cell attended by new people who have little knowledge and no development. Here, the task is to consolidate and involve the people in a process of personal transformation. Many are called, and evangelistic discipleship work is begun.

Bringing forth more fruit (John 15:2). This is a cell attended by people with more knowledge of God's Word and who are more organized into the vision. Most of them are training for leadership.

Bringing forth much fruit (John 15:5). This stage is reached when all attendees are prepared for multiplication, i.e., twelve new cells. The group, already developed, goes through a time of preparation with the objective in mind, of what they must do, to be sent afterwards. Every cell vision must bear fruit and is reflected in the number of cells that are periodically started. We know that in all effort there is fruit and this must be kept mindful from the very beginning.

FOURTH COMMANDMENT:
MEET ONCE A WEEK

The best frequency for cell meetings is weekly. The leader and the host as well as the other members of the cell must work to bring new people into each meeting. When Cornelius received Peter's visit, he represented a cell leader. He prepared by extending the invitation to his family and close friends who contributed to the success of that meeting. The Holy Spirit was poured out for the first time to a group of non-Jews, leaving all of Peter's companions astounded seeing how God blessed them in the same way that they had been blessed.

Do not allow this weekly cell meeting to stray its intended purpose. Try always to maintain a good spiritual balance and avoid mysticism.

The vision of the church is reproduced within these cells. These meetings should be homogeneous: men with men, women with women, youth with youth, couples with couples and children with children. This way people who speak the "same language" can develop a more effective work.

FIFTH COMMANDMENT:
CELLS MUST HELP IN FAMILY RESTORATION

Cellular work is meant to restore families. The entire world is being shaken by family crisis. Wherever we go we find that people need answers to solve family problems, whether it being, between couples or between parents and children.

The cell must be prepared to tend these needs. In the cells, we seek to restore relationships between children and their parents, and husbands and their wives. Success with this task requires discerning of Spirits to get to the root of problems, to heal deep wounds of the soul and to break the chains that bind them from the past.

In the cell, the families are seen as small churches, we minister with the intention of reaffirming the blood ties and the preeminence of love among each family member. We are convinced that the basis for restoring society is to restore its principal nucleus, the family. This requires the fulfillment of all processes that allow rebirth of one's life and family to mature, and practicing each stage in the proper order. Paul says, *"Let all things be done decently and in order"* (I Corinthians 14:40).

If anyone needs a deeper ministry, we suggest that that person be taken to a 3-day Encounter during which he will undergo deliverance, inner healing, assurance of salvation and infilling of the Holy Spirit.

SIXTH COMMANDMENT:
MAKE A LEADER OF EACH MEMBER

People with diverse needs come to church and the same opportunities must be presented to each individual so that they can reach spiritual maturity. We must learn to see them with eyes of faith. I suggest that each person who visits a cell, be visualized as a great leader. You don't know if that person may become a champion for winning souls and starting cells. We have heard testimonies of particular individuals won to the Lord and their lives and testimonies have been used to change multitudes, even entire nations.

SEVENTH COMMANDMENT:
GUARD THE GROUP'S SANCTITY

The Lord's doctrine of sanctity is summarized: *"I am holy, and without holiness, no one will see me."* When sin is allowed, tolerated and consented, immediately the cell begins to deteriorate. You must have a radical attitude against sin and not entrust cells to someone who leads a double life because a leader's *letter of guarantee* must be his testimony. Sanctity must begin with the leader and he must guard against even the smallest of indiscretions. Solomon understood that, *"The little foxes spoil the vines."* The testimony of the leader starts in his own home, and he must have a house of peace in which the presence of Christ reigns and makes all efforts for his family members to live in the fear of the Lord.

Living in sanctity is possible when we are ready to confess our mistakes. If someone falls, the first one to know it must be your leader or pastor. One of the members of my team was asked, *"If you sinned, which person would you tell first?"* He answered, *"My pastor."* The one who asked the question was an evangelist who was surprised by the answer because, generally, the one whom the fallen leader would least likely want to know would be his pastor.

However, we have established friendships with our leadership, which has nurtured trust and closeness between us, consequently it is possible to receive to restoration to recover sanctity.

EIGHTH COMMANDMENT:
DO NOT BUILD ON ANOTHER'S FOUNDATION

In our congregation, we have encountered cases of people who thought that by attracting a leader from another ministry they were saving time. But our experience has shown to the contrary. The only thing they have achieved has been to delay the process of development.

For example, once, the International Men's Net ecstatically reported a great number of cells. But I noticed that most of their members were woman and they complained that the men didn't want to commit.

I made the decision to have the men hand over the women in their cells to their respective wives, which proved to be a great help to them. Each member must be faithful to his own cell and should not visit different cells, since this may cause confusion and he will not be able to enter into the required process of his ministerial development.

You should not fill your cell with members of other churches because this creates instability in those people.

NINTH COMMANDMENT:
DO NOT PERMIT MURMURING INSIDE THE CELL

When water stagnates it decomposes, reeks and generates bad odors. When a cell stagnates and doesn't grow it goes through the same process.

The consequences are gossip, murmuring, criticism and complaining.

Never allow someone to speak badly about another. A preacher who visited us years ago said, *"If I have nothing good to say about someone, I prefer to say nothing."* Guard your tongue and never murmur about the pastor, the leaders or the church. If you see defects or weaknesses in others, pray because maybe the Lord is placing a burden of prayer on you for them.

Remember that all of the Israelites who murmured while wandering through the desert were left abandoned and never entered the Promised Land. When murmuring begins, it results in devastation. Be radical, never allow gossipers into your cell.

TENTH COMMANDMENT:
DEVELOP YOUR GOALS STRATEGICALLY

It is important to have achievable goals, but that requires effort on your part. Your goals must be clear and with the purpose of multiplication. Never establish goals with a negative mentality, thinking that it is going to be difficult to achieve them. You must be ready to assume the risks that the vision demands. Develop a program of written goals of all your objectives as this will help maintain a spirit of prayer in support of those goals, and do not give up until they are achieved.

It is important to:

- Commit to achieving them.
- Supervise them continually.
- Keep in physical, spiritual and mental shape.
- Turn your disadvantages into advantages.
- Maintain a disciplined life.

- Acquire as much assistance as possible.
- Work as a team.
- Be positive.
- Dream with success.

The work of the church must be like a business, with targeted projections. If we talk to a manager of a company about his goals, he will show us a chart with projections that he desires to reach. However, when we talk with many leaders and pastors about their projections, the answer often is, *"My church's projection is to do what God wants me to do."* That's not right. When God gives you a vision you become like the pilot of a plane and must know where you are going. If the pastor doesn't have the vision, neither does his church. The leader must know the vision of the Twelve and how he is going to prepare his people, how many cells he should have by year's end, et cetera. Consider that great achievements begin by the conquest of small goals. God fulfills His goals using members of His church.

Chapter Seven

A LADDER TO SUCCESS

"Possess the virtue of powerful spiritual strength that is overcoming and energetic, since the world needs people who are aggressive in the Word, strong of spirit, and who are worth imitating." C.C.D.

THE INNER CORE OF THE VISION

Currently, the application of the principles of the vision allows us to obtain greater results than in the beginning. The Lord has brought us to the creation of a process that guarantees success to everyone who is ready to consecrate oneself to cell work. We call this process the LADDER OF SUCCESS. There are four steps, which when followed in order, make a leader of every new believer and transform him into an agent of multiplication, able to expand the vision of Christ's message.

These four steps are: WIN, CONSOLIDATE, DISCIPLE, SEND.

Each one of these steps is linked and intertwined with the other. That is the only way to produce results. More than 150 years ago, Justus von Liebig, biologist and chemist, discovered that for plant development and fruit bearing there must be four fundamental elements; nitrogen, potassium, lime and phosphoric acid. If one of the chemical elements in the soil is used in a greater proportion than the other, you will not get the same result. Now, referring to the steps in the Ladder of Success, some may dedicate far more time discipling in the School of Leaders and neglect the consolidation, or may spend much time consolidating, while neglecting evangelism. This is how you get the best fruit. Optimum results are obtained when each step develops in balance with the other until completing the cycle. Since our intention is to guide you in the best possible way for implementing your cell vision, I will deal with each step of the Ladder of Success so that it brings you abundant fruit.

Some of the items discussed in this section have already been previously mentioned in the other chapters, however to fully grasp this vision in its fullness, repetition is necessary and the overlapping of the subject matter is inevitable. Next, I will talk about the first step.

THE CHALLENGE IS TO WIN SOULS

"And Jesus came and spoke to them, saying, all authority has been given to Me in heaven and on earth. Go therefore and make disciples of all nations, baptizing them in the name of the Father and the Son and of the Holy Spirit."
(*Matthew* 28:18-19)

In its simplest form, evangelism is realized in either a personal way, as when we establish direct contact with those to whom we desire to win for Christ by taking advantage of all possible social situations, or, in the much larger format of local church meetings, the alter call. Evangelism is the first stage of the Ladder and guarantees success to the cell vision, because without evangelism we will not have anyone to introduce to the cells. The task of winning lost souls is not optional, it is a process that the Lord established as vital and essential so that the world may know him and experience his eternal salvation.

> *"And this is life eternal, that they might know You, the only true God, and Jesus Christ whom You have sent."* (John 17:3)

In the first stage of winning souls, our duty is to take people through the process of introducing them to the gospel. In addition, we must also decontaminate them from gods they may have served, enabling them know the true God and Jesus Christ, and to enter into the dimension of eternal life. To communicate the gospel to the world, an entire army is needed. The angels could easily achieve this, but this privilege was entrusted to us who have been redeemed by the blood of the Lamb. Angels are at the disposal as God's servants and are ministering agents whom the Lord placed as our collaborators in the valiant work of evangelism.

> *"...And valiant men went with him, whose hearts God had touched."* (1 Samuel 10:26b)

Those who accompanied Saul were men of war but they also possessed renewed hearts, which had been touched by God. Within the work developed by the International Charismatic Mission, our people are highly committed to evangelization and they do it with zeal and great compassion. I observe that they too, are men and women of war because God has already prepared their hearts. To have that kind of army you must start with a very simple yet effective concept, person-to-person evangelism.

IT IS A STRATEGY

The Lord showed us a great strategy to win souls with the story of the Samaritan woman: *From one personal dialogue came salvation for a whole city.* He told His disciples, *"Do you not say, 'There are still four months and then comes the harvest?' Behold, I say to you, lift up your eyes and look at the fields, for they are already white for harvest."*
(John 4:35)

The Lord declares that there is no time to lose when fruit is ripe on the tree. If the reapers don't harvest it soon it will fall to the ground and be lost. People can harden their hearts and then a much stronger effort will be required. How many nations have let the time of God's grace pass and didn't harvest because they felt satisfied? Some leaders say, *"We already have 500 or 1,000 people in our congregation, this is revival!"* They stopped their evangelistic work and hearts were hardened. Thank God that Colombia is living in one of its best times, because even amid adversity God has placed His hand over our nation and has blessed us with an abundant harvest of souls. Everyone who comes to Colombia says, *"This is a time of the grace of God for this nation."* Wherever you preach and to whomever you speak, their hearts are open to accept Christ.

THE HARVEST IS READY

"And he who reaps receives wages, and gathers fruit for eternal life, that both he who sows and he who reaps may rejoice together. For in this the saying is true: 'One sows, and another reaps.'"(John 4:36-37)

The Lord teaches that some preach but don't see conversions. Nevertheless, they spread the seed.

Others preach and the people convert. But that conversion was not the result of a work done at that time because others have already left the field fertilized. They prepared the soil of people's hearts so that when another arrived he simply took the fruit and consolidated it. The Lord also shows that whoever plants will not go un-rewarded even if he doesn't see the fruits of conversion.

"I have sent you to reap that for which you have not labored and you have entered into their labors. (John 4:38)

How many evangelistic methods have existed? Many have existed and have been fruitful. But grace has always been present to implement a Divine strategy to take the fruit, consolidate and retain it so that it would produce more. Many have not understood this step in the evangelism process. We cannot stop working with what God has entrusted us. This is our primary vision.

After reviewing person-to-person evangelism, I indeed thank God that our people are being trained to reproduce Christ's character wherever they find themselves. For example, as senior pastor I cannot be at all company businesses in my community. Members of my church are there. I trained them so that they can do the evangelistic work at their work, schools and universities and in their neighborhoods. Training people is a vital part of the work that God has entrusted us.

English preacher, Charles Spurgeon, said, *"If I was an absolute egotist and worried for nothing except my own happiness, even then I would worry to win souls for Christ; because I never knew a most indescribable, pure and bursting happiness than the one that filled me the day I saw someone who had found his Savior by my means, or for her first-born nor any warrior has exalted more after obtaining a victory.*" Spurgeon had never experienced so much joy in his life, as when he saw one soul surrendering before Christ's feet through one of his messages. This happens when one is a channel of blessing to others and becomes the instrument that God uses to snatch a person out of the dark abyss and transfers him into the Kingdom of Christ.

A young man, eleven years old and the son of a leader of the couple's group had a dream related to the Apocalypse. He saw how souls were going to perdition. He also saw the beast that Revelation talks about, a worldwide religious leader behind which there was a beast with seven heads. It was a terrible monster. He saw how people were being cheated, and were on their way to hell. He saw the lake of fire and that when people fell into it, their skin would come off as if acid was being poured on them. This young man had never read the book of Revelation. God gave him this revelation so that he would feel compassion for lost souls. Simultaneously, the Lord showed him the happiness of God's heavenly kingdom and he could see that what the Bible teaches is indeed a great reality.

American evangelist, R.A. Torrey, testified, *"I knew little of the joy of salvation until someone accepted Christ for the first time through me. What do you feel when someone converts? We should never lose the joy of seeing people surrendering their lives to Christ."*

WE WIN WHILE WE BATTLE

Paul said, *"To the weak I became as weak, that I might gain the weak. I have become all things to all men, that I might by all means save some"* (1 Corinthians 9:22). Paul does not limit the gospel as he sets out to be an effective strategist to be able to reach as many as possible regardless of their social position, cultural status or racial origin.

"...And he who wins souls is wise." (Proverbs 11:30b)

The Bible doesn't say that whoever makes money is wise, nor does it say whomever studies much is wise, no only those who win souls are wise.

"Who desires all men to be saved and to come to the knowledge of the truth." (1 Timothy 2:4)

I believe that when the land is fertilized it can be cultivated and if adequate seed has been planted, fruit will be seen. American evangelist, Dwight L. Moody, heard the preacher, Henry Barley, say, *"The world has not seen what God can do with a man completely surrendered to Him."* This message changed his life and he decided, that that man was going to be him. He became one of America's greatest soul winners. A man totally surrendered in the hands of God is someone who can transform entire nations for the glory of the Lord Jesus Christ.

"I beseech you therefore, brethren, by the mercies of God that you present your bodies a living sacrifice, holy, acceptable to God, which is your reasonable service. And do not be conformed to this world, but be transformed by the renewing of your mind, that you may prove what is that good and acceptable and perfect will of God."(Romans 12:1-2)

What is the apostle saying here? He is imploring us to present our bodies a living sacrifice, holy and pleasing to the Lord, namely, a daily life lived with the integrity and uprightness of a leader. Furthermore, the leader must continually renew his mind, which is a process. This renovation happens when we are at God's alter dying everyday to our selfish desires and further, it is where we confirm God's will which is to win souls. His good will is pleasing and perfect.

"Or do you not know that your body is the temple of the Holy Spirit who is in you, whom you have from God, and you are not your own? For you were bought at a price; therefore glorify God in your body and in your spirit, which are God's" (1 Corinthians 6:19-20)

The Lord paid a huge price for each individual soul, and it was the price of His blood on the cross of Calvary. Two thousand years ago, Jesus paid for that very soul to whom you are witnessing God's love. That is the message we must share and if they believe it, they will be translated from darkness into the kingdom of His dear Son. That is when that dear individual becomes the temple of the Holy Spirit.

"Fear not, for I am with you; I will bring your descendents from the east, and gather you from the west; I will say to the north, 'Give them up!' And to the south, 'Do not keep them back!' Bring my sons from afar, and my daughters from the ends of the earth." (Isaiah 43:5-6)

As a local church, we take authority over demonic powers, binding the spirits that operate in the spiritual realm over the north, south, east and west and ordering them to release the souls that are bound, in the name of Jesus. Then we activate the angels, asking them to prepare souls to receive our gospel message. First, you must win the war against the devil in the secret place, moving your local church towards spiritual warfare. You then send workers to different sectors to evangelize because your opposition has been removed. Finally, you restore souls to the knowledge of God's truth.

Chapter Eight

CONSOLIDATE

"Sanctity is God's fingerprint, faith relates you to Him, and diligence will make you a participant at his table." C.C.D.

CONSERVATION OF THE FRUIT

The church of the Lord was established with a firm foundation: Jesus Christ as the chief cornerstone, over which all the weight of the church would rest.

"For no other foundation can anyone lay than which is laid, which is Jesus Christ." (1 Corinthians 3:11)

The apostolic and prophetic foundations would gradually be placed over this chief base, confirmed in (Ephesians 2: 20)

"...having been built on the foundation of the apostles and prophets, Jesus Christ Himself being the chief corner stone."

Afterwards, a special grace would come through which God's Spirit would be in charge of the perfect coordination of its growth, until reaching the maturity of a holy temple for the Lord.

"...in whom the whole building, being fitted together, grows into a holy temple in the Lord, in whom you also are being built together for a dwelling place of God in the Spirit."(Ephesians 2:21-22)

The spiritual development of each believer requires total surrender to God's Spirit because in the spiritual sense we are living stones, and the Holy Spirit is in charge of placing each stone in its proper position. In this plan the Lord requires that each person, be molded by His Spirit. This shaping is gradually defined, until that person has been won for Christ, in a process called *consolidation*. Consolidation, the efficient process of forming disciples, is the stage where the new believer *reaffirms* his personal decision for Jesus Christ, which is achieved through the care given to that person right at the moment of surrender.

In a conversation I had with a well-known evangelist, he told me, *"During the 1980's about 2,000,000 people converted in our crusades, and today I need 5,000 ushers to support us in our evangelistic events but the pastors cannot find them. Where are the people that we have won?"* The anxiety of this evangelist is the same experienced in hundreds of churches around the world. Of all the people who have passed this way, how many have stayed in church? As a collective urban transport vehicle, the people enter the church by the front door, stay for a short time, and leave out the back door. The reason for this phenomenon is failure to conserve the fruit. There is no effective program of *consolidation*, i.e., a program to help shut the back door.

The Lord made us aware of the need to take care of new believers by offering them guidelines to help affirm their Christian faith and their commitment to Christ and the church. In this regard, we have tried to strengthen them so that each one who surrenders his heart in the meetings stays in the local church and even trains to be a leader to win others.

In our church, a weekly average of 1,000 to 1,500 people surrender their lives to Jesus. We count on a team of consolidators that take them to a separate room to help them reaffirm the step they have taken, giving them basic principles of the Christian life. Afterwards, they are prepared for discipleship. They are then taken to a 3-day *ENCOUNTER*. Afterwards, they are linked to a cell and finally they are established in the School of Leaders. It takes about six months to develop a person. But *consolidation* achieves this objective and the new believer is ushered into the reaffirmation of his faith and commitment to the Lord.

AVOID BARRENNESS

Paul writes to Timothy in his letter, Chapter 2, verse 15, and makes an allegory of the church with a woman, *"Nevertheless she will be saved in childbearing, if they continue in faith, love and holiness, with self-control."* However, there are many barren churches in the world today that have spent years with that same membership, not only because they have not done continuous and aggressive evangelistic work, but because they have not taken care to consolidate their fruit. Avoid barrenness.

WITHOUT BIRTH THERE IS NO MULTIPLICATION

The apostle Paul won souls with much exertion, weeping, and shedding of tears. That's why we read in Galatians 4: 19, *"My little children, for whom I labor in birth again until Christ is formed in you."*

Without experiencing the labor pains of the new birth, there cannot be consolidation. The Lord tells Sidon, *"Be ashamed, O Sidon; for the sea has spoken, the strength of the sea, saying, 'I do not labor, nor bring forth children; neither do I rear young men, nor bring up virgins'"* (Isaiah 23:4). Sidon represents some churches that have never experienced labor pains in their ministry and therefore have not borne children, namely, they have not been fruitful and there has not been multiplication in their work.

THE BARRENNESS OF THE FIG TREE

"He also spoke this parable: A certain man had a fig tree planted in his vineyard, and he came seeking fruit on it and found none. Then he said to the keeper of his vineyard, 'Look for three years I have come seeking fruit on this fig tree and find none. Cut it down; why does it use up the ground?' But he answered and said to him, 'Sir let it alone this year also, until I dig around it and fertilize it. And if it bears fruit, well. But if not, after that you can cut it down." (*Luke* 13:6-9)

There are many interpretations of this parable, but I see it in the context of the local church. The vineyard, in general, is the Lord's church and the fig tree is the local church. The Lord looks for fruit, but doesn't find any so He tells His vineyard keeper to, *"Cut it!"* This means to withdraw God's grace from that church, but then a new opportunity is given. Prophets and servants ready to do the work with a new strategy of growth are sent in to see if it will bear fruit. We see the complement to this account in Matthew 21:19. There, the Lord approaches the fig tree to look for fruit. He doesn't find any so he orders it to become barren. In the same way, Jesus arrives at our local churches expecting to feed from the fruit that should be there, represented by the lives that have been born again and transformed, but He cuts it down if He finds none.

Something interesting to note is this teaching is that the fig tree was on the roadside. There are churches that have not entered the Lord's vineyard, but have only stayed nearby. That's why they have not been fruitful. Everything next to the road dries. It is necessary for the church to form part of the Lord's vineyard. If your church had been barren God offers a new opportunity, declaring, *"'Sing, O, barren, you who have not borne! Break forth into singing, and cry aloud, you who have not labored with child! For more are the children of the desolate than the children of the married woman,' says the Lord"* (Isaiah 54:1). Here, God indicates that times of great growth and multiplication for the church are coming, after the people are born again in Christ's gospel and cared for through consolidation, which indeed gives them guidelines to walk firmly in the truth.

FIVE STAGES OF GROWTH FOR EACH PERSON

Consolidation is then that stage which follows the *surrender* to the Lordship of Christ, where the new convert receives careful attention until Christ's character is fully reproduced in him. Jesus Christ, with the support of His Twelve, was the best consolidator and in praying for His team in John 17, showed five stages of growth that must develop in the life of the believer, just as with His own disciples:

REVELATION OF THE SCRIPTURES

"I have manifested Your name to the men whom You have given me out of the world. They were Yours, You gave them to Me, and they have kept Your word" (John 17:6). The first step has to deal with the revelation of the Scriptures and is an exposition clearly understood by the people. The message is grasped without interruptions or doubts.

295

God's Word then becomes *rhema* and light to them, and the new believer goes on to form part of the fellowship.

DISCIPLESHIP IN THE SCHOOL OF LEADERS

"For I have given to them the words which You have given Me; and they have received them, and have known surely that I came forth from You, and they have believed that You sent me" (John 17:8). This means that the teachings t.1at God has given to the leaders are shared with the new coverts in a methodical way. This process has been established in the School of Leaders where each one is formed until development in this level of ministry is matured.

FORMATION OF CHARACTER THROUGH THE WORD

"I have given them Your Word; and the world has hated them because they are not of the world, just as I am not of the world" (John 17:14). Every believer is going to be attacked by the world, his family, friends and even acquaintances. These people rise against the new believer loathing and despising him. That's when the new convert must be strengthened and developed in Christ's character. Your work is to teach him that he doesn't belong to this world anymore and therefore, he cannot allow the attacks to affect him.

SPIRITUAL MATURITY

"Sanctify them by Your truth. Your word is truth" (John 17:17).

When a person has overcome rejection his character is solid and he can enter through God's word into a season of intimate communion with God striving for personal sanctification.

THE MINISTERIAL LIFE

"I do not pray for these alone, but also for those who will believe in Me through their word" (John 17:20). The Lord prayed specifically for all those who reached out for His heavenly kingdom, which is equivalent to their ministerial development within God's mission. Each person that has experienced a personal encounter with Jesus Christ must understand that he didn't choose God, God chose him that he may produce fruit relative to God's mission, *"You did not choose Me, but I chose you and appointed you that you should go and bear fruit, and that your fruit should remain"* (John 15:16).

The beginning of *consolidation* is also found in Acts, Chapter 2, where the account of the apostle Peter, inspired by the Holy Spirit, delivered an excellent dissertation focusing on the following points:

The Holy Spirit outpouring upon all flesh would fall on the sons, daughters, young, elderly and servants, of both men and women, with many signs following. This was to occur before the return of Christ on earth. On earth these signs would be of blood, fire, smoke, and vapor in the sky and the sun would darken and the moon would turn red.

The earthly ministry of Jesus was supernatural and accompanied with signs and wonders. He died, was raised, ascended to heaven, and will return when the Father subdues all His enemies under His feet. This Jesus, whom the people of Israel crucified, was established as Lord and Christ.

Acts 2:37 says that when those present heard Peter's message, they were cut to the heart with compunction and asked the apostle what to do. Matthew Henry comments that the audience felt sharp pricks in their conscience when they heard the message, because in the Greek, *compunction* means to feel pricks in the heart. The message pierced deeply because of the anointing of the preacher. It wasn't something that remained in the intellect but it reached their souls. That's why they asked, *"What must we do to be saved?"* Peter replies, *"Repent, and let every one of you be baptized in the name of Jesus Christ for the remission of sins, and you shall receive the gift of the Holy Spirit"* (Acts 2:38).

Peter talks about repentance as a change of heart in the course of one's life. The course of action that follows is baptism, as the burial of one's past life, i.e., an act of faith in which people do not have to be crucified for their sins but confirm their decision to accept Christ's sacrifice for them. As they rise out of the water the Holy Spirit is received. Paul teaches the Galatians, *"For as many of you as were baptized into Christ have put on Christ'* (Galatians 3:27). Following Peter's preaching, 3,000 people were converted.

According to commentator Matthew Henry, this could be considered a multiplication miracle, even greater than the loaves and fishes. The phrase *attached* or *added* in Acts 2: 47 suggests that those who were won were incorporated as part of the family of the new church. The apostles performed a *consolidation* during this time by ensuring that new converts were baptized in water and given the opportunity to receive the baptism in the Holy Spirit with evidence, if speaking in tongues and further ensured that they received healthy doctrine for their edification and an anointing to preach the gospel. *"And they continued steadfastly in the apostles' doctrine and fellowship, in breaking of bread, and in prayers"* (Acts 2:42).

In this chapter we have only in general terms the beginning of *consolidation* which establishes a biblical orientation, and the fundamentals of *"why"* and *"what for"* in this stage of the Ladder to Success. In the next chapter we will learn important aspects about the consolidator and the process.

Chapter Nine

THE CONSOLIDATOR
AND HIS PROCESS

"The renewing of the mind gets man out of the conventional causing him to explore a completely different world full of emotional, edifying, and pleasing adventures."
C.C.D.

STEP BY STEP UNTIL VICTORY IS ACHIEVED

Consolidation produces effective results when there is someone committed to developing it by following each step of the process. Every person who gets involved as a consolidator must know that his mission is to care for the new believer, reproduce Christ's character in him so that he may produce fruit, reproducing it in others. This task requires much effort, consecration, and dedication. But this task above all, requires love for souls, which are the dearest to God's heart.

We cannot forget that the great Commission goes further than simply winning souls; because this is only the first step. The next requirement is to convert each one to be a disciple of Christ. With consolidation we seek to establish a life change in every person. This requires men and women who are willing to supervise the day-by-day progress of the newly converted.

PRINCIPLES THAT SHOULD
RULE CONSOLIDATION

"Then those who gladly received his word were baptized; and that day about three thousand souls were added to them. And they continued steadfastly in the apostles' doctrine and fellowship, in breaking of bread, and in prayers." "...And the Lord added to the church daily those who were being saved."(Acts 2:41-42, 47).

From this text we extract the following principles: Verifying the surrender, indoctrinating the new believer, camaraderie or fellowship, sanctity and prayer.

VERIFYING THE SURRENDER

One of the ways the adversary tries to rob the new convert of what he has received is by affecting his understanding. In other words, the person may fight against himself, his pride, criticism, against his family, et cetera. The work of the consolidator in this case is to take each new believer and help him to understand what is happening in his life. This part is fulfilled by taking the new believer into a separate room after his prayer of faith and public confession of receiving Christ as Lord and Savior. In this room, each one is asked if they understood why Jesus is now in their hearts. An illustrated exposition should be given about the meaning of this decision and then he is invited to reaffirm his decision.

At the moment of verification of the surrender essential data of each person, such as name, address, telephone number, activities and fundamental needs are written on a card to be later codified and distributed among the group of consolidators.

We do not work by geographic zones because we found that when the area of work was limited by geography we had too many problems. Each new convert should therefore be placed where he can reach his spiritual growth and leadership projections. The consolidator who receives the card should have a cell in the sector where the new convert lives to enable his care. More than a card, the consolidator is receiving a life and soul who is being born into God's spiritual kingdom.

INDOCTRINATING THE NEW BELIEVER

"And they continued steadfastly in the apostle's doctrine..." (Acts 2:42). To indoctrinate means to teach a new way of life. The newly converted must be trained in a diligent way until he learns to live the Christian life. The apostles were always concerned about the need to share the sacred Scriptures and Christ's doctrine among their new disciples, teaching them in the temple and in homes.

Since the indoctrination of the new believer requires diligence, implementing this process must be started very quickly. Just as a newborn baby cannot wait eight days to be fed neither can the spiritual newborn baby wait eight days to be fed. The spiritual baby requires immediate nourishment. We suggest doing this within 48 hours of surrendering his life to Christ, with the objective of obtaining defined fruit during that indoctrination period. Teaching the new believer without seeing the corresponding fruit doesn't make sense.

When we indoctrinate we look for change in the life of each person because we are forming the leaders, we're creating new people. The following summarizes the apostles' work of indoctrination and their success: *"And when they had preached the gospel to that city and made many disciples, they returned to Lystra, Iconium, and Antioch, strengthening the souls of the disciples, exhorting them to continue in the faith, and saying, 'We must through many tribulations enter the kingdom of God.' So when they had appointed elders in every church, and prayed with fasting, they commended them to the Lord in whom they had believed"* (Acts 14:21-23). This should motivate us to do the same. The results are extraordinary. When we see the new convert become a pillar in the development of the church's vision, it produces a great satisfaction.

FELLOWSHIP AND CAMARADERIE

"And they continued steadfastly in the apostles' doctrine and <u>fellowship</u> and in breaking of bread, and in prayers." Here is a clear idea of the fellowship that allowed the believers of the early church to have the sense of belonging to a group.

God created us as social beings and he enjoys it when there is a common union between brethren. People who come into a church environment from the secular world, where perhaps they have had various types of relationships with non-Christians, need to relate to those who have a higher spiritual level to help them grow and transition into their new life in Christ.

Fellowship also requires perseverance. We must ensure that the objective of communion is achieved. When many start their Christian life they tend to isolate themselves from the group to pray, read the Bible and consecrate themselves at home, and may neglect the importance of communion with the brethren. I have known of places in other nations where believers don't even assemble at church anymore, but stay at home receiving sermons by radio or television. This results in loss of communion blessing. Radio and television programs are valuable for edifying the believer but they can never replace the interaction of fellowship. The psalmist says, *"Behold, how good and how pleasant it is for brethren to dwell together in unity. For there the Lord commanded the blessing, life for evermore"* (Psalm 133:1,3b).

GUARD SANCTITY

"And they continued steadfastly in the apostles' doctrine and fellowship, <u>and in breaking of bread,</u> and in prayers." The tendency may be to think exclusively on the idea of sharing natural food, but the text goes further than that. It concerns the sharing of spiritual bread. At that moment, the apostles were sharing the Lord's Supper and this experience implied lives of sanctification.

With regard to the Lord's Supper, the apostle Paul imparts precise instructions about the state of each person who desires to participate in this important celebration. Paul says that each one must examine oneself and conclude if they are worthy or not to be a part of the Lord's table. If your conscience accuses you because there is hidden sin in your life it is better that you abstain from participating, otherwise you would be eating and drinking judgment on yourself (1 Corinthians 11:29). But if your self-examination results in peace because you have kept your life pure then you can participate without any difficulties.

PERSEVERE IN PRAYER

"And they continued steadfastly in the apostles' doctrine and fellowship, and in breaking of bread, <u>and in prayers</u>." Dr. Joe Johns, a Christian minister, comments that you can only pray together with those having the same faith and same love. Others always looked upon the disciples as being men of prayer, and this caused the new believer to assume the same habit. In the consolidation process prayer moves the hand of God in favor of the people. It is the key to unleashing the power of the Holy Spirit in each life and bringing growth to the church. Each objective is achieved through persevering prayer. Our desire in the natural realm must be conquered through prayer in the spiritual realm.

In addition to these principles, the consolidator must consider the importance of adequate preparation for the work of preserving the fruit. God is placing His anointing upon common people to reach out to the world. But if we are not prepared we will have problems for which we must answer to God. I believe that if we aspire to a large ministry we must be willing to learn and prepare ourselves. The preparation to be effective consolidators includes five things. (Note again, some of the items referenced below have been discussed in earlier chapters, but because of their importance and for continuity, they bear repeating).

1. Integrity. God chooses people based on the attitude of their hearts. When He sees that they adhere to His ethics and moral principles and do not abandon them under any circumstances, He then releases power on them for His service. When the Lord sees sanctity in the heart of a man He puts a unique and powerful touch on his ministry giving him the opportunity to reap abundant fruit. We will never see fruit

if there is no integrity in our lives and we do not walk wholly after Him, *"Surely none of the men who came up from Egypt, from twenty years old and above, shall see the land of which I swore to Abraham, Isaac, and Jacob, because they have not wholly followed Me, except Caleb the son of Jephunneh, the Kenezzite, and Joshua the son of Nun, for they have wholly followed the Lord"* (Numbers 32:11-12).

2. Deep compassion for the people. The same compassion that Christ felt for the needy is what the consolidator must have for those entrusted to him. Paul said,

"That I have sorrow and continual grief in my heart. For I could wish that I myself were accursed from Christ for my brethren, my countrymen according to the flesh."
(Romans 9:2-3)

We see the apostle Paul's deep desire that his own race be saved, and this caused him to weep exceedingly. When writing to the Philippians, Paul says, *"For God my witness, how greatly I long for you all with the affection of Jesus Christ."* Compassion is at work when one weeps for the lost and once they are won, compassion gives them the care that they need. Remember, what you do not love you do not minister to. We shut down the voice of the adversary by loving each person we come in contact with.

3. Trained in using the Word of God. The consolidator must know that we do not change someone because we have an aptitude for words or charisma. What changes people is the Word of God and power of the Spirit working in their hearts. Every person who cares for a new convert must be prepared in the use of Scriptures, familiarizing himself with the necessary texts to share with those in his charge. God's Word is our principle weapon to defeat the enemy and only through it will we come to know God well.

4. **Permanent disposition.** The consolidator must be enterprising and diligent with a permanent disposition towards the mission. Paul tells Timothy, *"Be diligent to present yourself approved to God, a worker who does not need to be ashamed, rightly dividing the word of truth"* (2 Timothy 2:15).

Many people unfortunately live their lives and guide others exclusively by momentary feelings. James' epistle suggests that we cannot be like waves of the sea that are tossed to and fro one place to the next without becoming unstable.

5. **Importance of prayer.** The consolidator must pay the price in prayer for others because nothing is achieved without it. Explaining the model, Jesus said,

"But you, when you pray, go into your room, and when you have shut your door, pray to your Father who is in the secret place; and your Father who sees in secret will reward you openly." Matthew 6:6

Prayer must be dynamic, not monotonous, and it should move our hearts to reach God's heart. The prophet Daniel learned to use the secret of prayer and that is why he approached God with confidence looking for His favor for his people. In chapter Nine of the book of Daniel, we find in detail the way in which the prophet prayed for the Almighty's mercifulness for him and his people. Daniel identified with the sins of the people and asked forgiveness for them as if he had sinned. He recognized that his father's house had been rebellious and departed from the Divine commandments by disobeying the prophets. The curse had fallen over the people for their disobedience, but in his prayer, Daniel recognized that God was merciful and forgiving.

This is the type of prayer that must characterize the consolidator. He must substitute himself in place of the new believer and intercede for him until God's mercy brings conviction to motivate him to grow in his Christian walk.

Chapter Ten

DISCIPLE AND SEND

"The true encounter with Jesus produces recognition of authority, repentance form evil, a life of integrity, and the development of fruitful leadership." C.C.D

MAKING A LEADER OF EACH BELIEVER

The formation of leaders through the model of Twelve follows a solid program of training. It gives potential or prospective leaders the fundamental knowledge to evangelize and spread the vision. This is what resulted in the growth of the International Charismatic Mission. We are convinced that today the work of the church cannot be exclusively completed by the senior pastor, but only by working teams of the largest possible number of involved believers. Furthermore, the Lord removed the veil of limitation off our hearts for the preparation of our people. We have one objective: Daily, we strive to make each believer a leader.

The last two steps in the Ladder of Success help fulfill the purpose of formation and training: *Disciple* and *Send*. As in all the previous steps, these are intertwined, i.e., one takes you to the other. Believers are discipled in the School of Leaders where they are trained to win lost souls and exert positive leadership over their objectives, while reproducing Christ's character in each of their converts. It is a continuous cycle where everyone who receives Christ is trained so that others may in turn have a similar experience. It is therefore successive. We achieve our objective when each individual is trained in the Word of God and in understanding Christ's character. This will make him a faithful reflection of the Master. The Great Commission instructs us that we should *go and make disciples, teaching them to observe all things that God has commanded.*

Hosea 4:6 says, *"My people are destroyed for lack of knowledge. Because you have rejected knowledge, I will reject you from being priest for Me; because you have forgotten the law of your God, I also will forget your children."*

God gives us the opportunity to acquire the knowledge of His Word and gives us strategies that help share this knowledge with others.

DISCIPLESHIP

Our work cannot end after winning souls and then consolidating them, each one must be trained.

"For the equipping of the saints for the work of ministry, for the edifying of the body of Christ, till we all come to the unity of the faith and of the knowledge of the Son of God, to a perfect man, to the measure of the stature of the fullness of Christ; that we should no longer be children, tossed to and fro and carried about with every wind of doctrine, by the trickery of men, in the cunning craftiness of deceitful plotting, but, speaking the truth in love, may grow up into all things into Him who is the head, Christ, from whom the whole body, joined and knit together by what every joint supplies, according to the effective working by which every part does its share, causes growth of the body for the edifying of itself in love." (Ephesians 4:12-16)

For many years training was optional in our church. We asked our congregation who was interested in Biblical preparation, and discovered that very few wanted to commit for training. There wasn't interest in ministerial development with a defined leadership system. But when the Lord revealed the model of the Twelve to me I realized that whoever accepts Jesus Christ and commits to Him must also commit to His doctrine, and this demands training.

First, we carried out a program like the traditional biblical institute style, teaching hermeneutics, homiletics, eschatology, systematic theology, sects, et cetera. The results were not meeting the needs of our church because students filled their minds with knowledge, but were not demonstrating fruit in their lives. What we did was to copy other models, in which all who would lead a cell would prepare for two years. We started with a large group, but no more than 15 people finished the course. When they began to develop into leaders, they had no one to win because they had lost contact with most of their friends and acquaintances. Even their family members did not believe in them. Then God suggested that I strongly prepare the whole church and impart training that was not loaded with theology but with something more practical, and for the laity.

THE IMPORTANCE OF MAKING A
LEADER OF EACH BELIEVER

The Lord went on to show me the importance of making a leader of each member of the church and he gave me tools to train them. The School of leaders was begun and offered training for laity. We do not train in a formal manner using biblical and systematic theology. We emphasize the fundamental aspects of Christianity.

This required that we produce written materials that would satisfy our local needs, since the existing material we had, often conflicted with the vision we were developing as a church. So we began integrating basic principles of Christianity with principles of the vision and achieved outstanding results with our cell leaders.

Where we lacked or were weak in certain areas of training, the Lord gave us a strategy that allowed for the formation of each disciple and the training of leaders in a short time period. It is a theory-practical combination where a person in only six months starts bearing fruit while leading a cell. On one occasion I called four people to inquire about their ministerial development. Three of them were in the instruction program and that we had implemented, while the fourth was in the traditional system. The three who were linked to the School of Leaders had 90, 45 and 25 cells respectively, while the one who was in the other program only had 3 cells. Once again, I noticed that the previous system was too slow and had little strength. Those from the School of Leaders looked successful, dynamic and had the desire to keep multiplying, while the other one reflected a certain frustration caused by scarcity of fruit. Armed with this experience, I made the decision to strengthen the School of Leaders and gradually leave the previous program of instruction because of its institutionalized structure. That program, no longer exists today in our ministry.

INSTRUCTION HELPS TO ACHIEVE SUCCESS

.In the process of discipleship and instruction we help our leaders achieve success. The relationship that must exist between the leader and his disciples must be similar to the one between a father and his son, or the one that existed between Jesus and his disciples.

Something I've observed at the ministerial level that when pastors and leaders notice a person within their ranks rising and receiving recognition, they become filled with jealousy and fear and may even try to restrain his growth. A pastor may mistakenly believe that that disciple will grow larger than he is and eventually displace him. That's why we find many frustrated people whose opportunity to develop in ministry, was never given to them. And furthermore, in order not to cause strife with their pastor they accept conditions for ministry that he sets for them.

In the School of Leaders we give even more opportunities to each person so that he may develop a fruitful leadership style. Consider the strategic life of the shark, an animal that knows, how to easily change according to its circumstances. If placed in small confines, it grows an average of fifty to eighty centimeters, but if it is free to move in a much larger space such as the ocean, it can become several meters in length. Things, similar to the shark's life, occur in leadership. There are leaders who have extraordinary potential, but because their vision is too small they do not develop and their ministries are stunted.

If old schemes are discarded in order to enter a broader vision, leaders will be able to experience extraordinary results. The renewing of one's mind and an inclination to leave traditions by accepting innovation are important keys to having fruitful ministries. I am not suggesting for one to get up and go contrary to those leaders in authority. I want to motivate you towards a change based on the successful experiences we've had in our church so that you and your ministries grow while developing the vision God has given you. The School of leaders is innovative and allows you to achieve this purpose.

THE PRICE OF DISCIPLESHIP

In discipleship there is a price to be paid, but there is great satisfaction when you see the change God brings in each life. It is therefore necessary for each leader to be ready to do five things.

Renounce. *"If anyone comes to Me and does not hate his father and mother, wife and children, brothers and sisters, yes, and his own life also, he cannot be My disciple"* (Luke 14: 26). In one incident, a man came to me and shared his family story, *"Pastor, my parents are Muslims and they forbade me to go back to the church, or they would disinherit me. But I told them that I didn't care if I lost everything, as long as I had the Lord in my life."* Perhaps some have heard their family tell them, *"You were born in our religious tradition and you cannot profane it."* But the courageous will answer, *"I am not a salve to tradition, because Jesus Christ set me free at the cross of Calvary."* No family member should ever be an obstacle to anyone who desires to commit oneself to the Lord.

Die daily. The Lord said, *" And whoever does not bear his cross and come after Me cannot be My disciple"* (Luke 14:27). This means that everyday you must go to the cross and be crucified with Christ. At the cross we must crucify our thoughts, emotions, desires, words, actions and all that could separate us from a genuine relationship with the Lord. If you don't do this, you are not worthy of being a disciple of Christ.

Have a vision of leadership. *"For which of you, intending to build a tower does not sit down first and count the cost, whether he has enough to finish it?"* (Luke 14:28).

Surely you know of people who have started a construction project or some other type of endeavor and have not finished it. When someone converts to Christ, what do you visualize him to be? You must see him as a great leader and must not give up under any circumstances until you see the work completed in him.

Persevere. *"Lest, after he has laid the foundation, and is not able to finish, all who see it begin to mock him, saying, 'This man began to build and was not able to finish'"* (Luke 14:29-30). Every disciple must have a good foundation. A good foundation occurs when work of excellent consolidation has been finished. You may win a person and consolidate him in the vision, but you must develop him until he becomes a disciple.

Engage in spiritual war for your disciples. *"Or what king, going to make war against another king, does not sit down first and consider whether he is able with ten thousand to meet him who comes against him with twenty thousand? Or else, while the other is still a great way off, he sends a delegation and asks conditions of peace"* (Luke 14:31-32). Understand winning souls implies engaging in spiritual war. You must be prepared to assess the forces of the adversary that arise against the formation of your disciples. You will have to face the demonic powers with full certainty that the ones with you are mightier than the ones who are against you. In this war, you battle for the salvation of each soul.

SEND THEM

The work of discipling to later send workers to field of action consists of molding each person and giving him spiritual and doctrinal nourishment until he becomes a valuable leader in the hands of God. This is comparable to the already stated anecdote of Michelangelo, the sculptor who took a piece of marble that another sculptor had rejected, visualized David in it, worked on it, and polished each area until <u>The David</u> surfaced on the stone.

Let's review some questions: Have you asked yourself what might the world have been like if Jesus Christ has not trained and poured His life into twelve men, and taught them His doctrine? Let's fast forward to the present: What might the world have been like if Billy Graham, or a woman like Kathryn Kulhman who changed people's lives with her ministry of miracles, had each trained 12 people?

The success of a ministry is sharing the vision with others who help develop it until it penetrates all spheres of a community. We have been doing it and declare to all who are preparing to work in this same important responsibility, that it works. When a disciple learns that he must increasingly give more of himself, this puts an obligation upon him. He then studies with more dedication and gradually comprehends that leadership is not awarded out of sympathy, but by merit.

Just as in the *Parable of the talents*, in the school of Leaders the disciple must put to work the natural ability that the Lord has given him and multiply it as was done by the one with five talents. People who are fruitful in that sense are the ones who are placed in higher levels of authority.

English Prime Minister, Winston Churchill, said before the House of Commons during the Second World War, *"I am your servant, you have the right to destroy me whenever you wish; what you don't have the right to do, is to give me responsibilities without giving me the power to act."* And it is that responsibility that contributes to authority.

Our leaders have authority over their disciples because they lead by example and by the testimony of their righteous lives.

When a leader acts irresponsibly by saying one thing and doing another, the disciple will soon recognize this and will relocate with another leader. But when the leader is responsible, all his disciples admire him and try to imitate his example. Johanna, my oldest daughter, whose leader is in the youth ministry, admires and appreciates him. Even though my opinion as her father is valuable to her, the guidance that she receives from her leader is primary. Johanna recognizes that I have a higher degree of authority because of my ministerial level. However, her leader has won her respect due to the testimony of his integrity, diligence, commitment, love for souls, jealousy for the things of God, his stand against sin and the development of the vision she sees in him. So she aspires to follow her leader's footsteps. That's what we expect to have happen with each person in our church, that he will be highly motivated by his leader. Leaders have the responsibility to serve as moral examples. We have achieved this with thousands and thousands of people who today make up a solid body of leaders in charge of our objectives in fulfilling the vision. The potential leader goes through the orderly steps of salvation, consolidation and discipleship, in preparation to be sent. But he initially goes through the *Pre-encounter*, and afterwards his *Encounter*, which are essential steps to free him of oppression and other bondages. Then he goes through training in the School of leaders where he will receive instructions and tools to help him fulfill his mission to lead a cell. Every believer who aspires to leadership must pass through these stages. These are important ways to accumulate your eternal riches, *"For where your treasure is, there your heart will be also"* (Matthew 6:21).

Furthermore, *"…if anyone not work, neither shall eat"* (2 Thessalonians 3:10). As a spiritual metaphor, if one does not work in God's mission, he will not enjoy the nourishment provided by Him, hence the importance of time invested in the preparation of your disciples.

Some pastors preach to entertain members of their church but do not develop or edify them. Jesus did not send us to entertain members of the church, He emphatically said, *"Go and make disciples."* Therefore, if someone does not accept the doctrine of the Lord do not invest your time in that person. The vision that we develop demands time invested in the formation of men and women who will ultimately bear fruit. As the parable teaches, if the owner of the vineyard comes and doesn't find fruit he will order it to be cut so as not to waste his land. The members of our church cannot be decorative or artificial plants; the fruit they bear must characterize them. After the serious work of discipling them is completed, each one is sent with the approval of their leader to lead a cell in God's vineyard.

Chapter Eleven

THE ENCOUNTER

"Everyone who has had a genuine encounter with Jesus will never be the same, his life is transformed and placed on a dimension of conquest." C.C.D.

A TRUE ENCOUNTER

To have an encounter with Jesus is the most extraordinary experience that can be had by a human being. Our life is transformed and our heart is renewed in the process. The spirit heightens, sadness disappears, pain vanishes and depression breaks apart because the strength of the Holy Spirit encourages us to keep going.

Therefore, we are willing to risk all to protect that which reveals to us the true meaning of life. Many, who have fought for the conquest of an illusion or fantasy, giving the appearance of reality, have ended up in disillusion and sadness because the unreal can never provide perfect happiness.

It is a fact that man is in search of happiness because he feels great emptiness in his heart. He tries to fill this emptiness in many ways; philosophy, education, sports, fame, money, pleasure, etcetera.

But as the years pass some realize that they have struggled in vain and remain spiritually empty. When God created man, He left a vacuum in his heart whose complement would make it whole and would be the secret of his happiness. That complement is the Lord Jesus Christ.

The patriarch Job exclaimed, *"Oh, that I knew where I might find Him, that I might come to His! I would present my cases before Him, and fill my mouth with arguments"* (Job 23:3-4).

Today, many live with the same anxiety as Job thinking that God is hidden somewhere in the Universe dedicated to His multiple occupations and that it is impossible to reach Him. That's why they exclaim, *"God where are you?"* They do not realize that He is closer to us than anyone can imagine. The apostle Paul said, *"...so that they should seek the Lord, in the hope that they might grope for Him and find Him, though He is not far from each one of us; for in Him we live and move and have our being, as also some of our own poets have said, 'For we are also His offspring"* (Acts 17:27-28).

In his dissertation to the Athenians, the apostle declares to anyone who desires, that it is not difficult to have an encounter with Christ because even with a simple examination we can find Him. He is as close to each one of us as the air that we breathe. The prophet Jeremiah says, *"And you will seek Me and find Me, when you search Me with all your heart"* (Jeremiah 29:13).

PREPARE FOR AN ENCOUNTER

For the new believer, the Encounter is a genuine event with Jesus Christ, the person of the Holy Spirit, and the sacred Scripture. The new convert is taken through repentance, deliverance of past ties and inner healing. The purpose is to impart clear guidance under the light of sacred Scriptures concerning his future in Jesus Christ. This is done through ministry on a personal and group level. Changes so important happen during that 3-day Encounter that attending it is equivalent to 1 year of Spiritual growth.

The new believer is prepared to develop an intimate relationship with the Lord, which aids him in learning prayer, reading of the Word and knowledge of the vision having these objectives in mind:

Motivate the new believer towards a genuine repentance and confession of his sins, taking him through the transforming experience of Calvary's cross to obtain all the benefits of being a son of God.

Look deep into his prenatal experiences, his childhood, adolescence and youth. With the guidance of the Holy Spirit and the Word of God, deliverance and inner healing can be ministered to the new believer, teaching him to keep a pure life before God.

Instruct the new believer in the apprenticeship of reading the Bible, prayer and communion with the Holy Spirit, guidance workshops and the practice of devotionals.

Guide the new Christian with practical tools so that he knows how to behave in his new lifestyle with his family and other relationships and respect for his own body, including what music to listen to and other lifestyle changes.

On his return from the Encounter, the new convert links with a cell. Later he will attend the Post-Encounter, where he will be guided with conferences and workshops to strengthen each teaching imparted in the Encounter. It will help him face his new change in relation to his family and establish friendship ties with other Christians who will support and pray continuously for him.

Finishing the Post-Encounter, the new believer will attend the School of Leaders where he will train in God's mission and where he will be able to climb towards the peak of success as a leader by getting to know the Lord Jesus Christ in a deeper way. At the school he is instructed with materials designed especially for him.

RENEWED MINDS AND TRANSFORMED LIVES

Most people who come to church are generally full of wounds, and if we set out to fill their minds with theology without first passing them through a process of restoration, it is as if a technical coach sends his athletes to the Olympics knowing that they have foot injuries. Similarly, in a previous world car championship, Canadian Greg Moore, a day before the final race suffered a slight fracture in one of his fingers. The doctors felt that there would not be a problem with his participation in the race. But it was impossible for him to keep control of the car because of his wounded finger and he hit a concrete wall. The accident traumatized millions of television spectators.

At the beginning of His ministry, Jesus said, *"The Spirit of the Lord is upon Me, because he has anointed me to preach the gospel to the poor; He has sent Me to heal the brokenhearted, to proclaim liberty to the captives and recovery of sight to the blind, to set at liberty those who are oppressed"* (Luke 4:18). It is the leader's duty to answer for the restoration of each person that the Lord sends in his community. The gospel that Jesus preached was an integral gospel, i.e., Jesus did not limit his activity to preaching the Good News. He also healed, delivered and restored people. The same must therefore happen in our Christian lives.

The vision we develop will not entertain members of the church, but will make a leader of each one if we follow Jesus' example. Since first being implemented, the Encounters have become a powerful tool in the vision by raising up a person, transforming him and giving him a new perspective of personal, spiritual and ministerial success.

HOW AND WHEN DOES AN ENCOUNTER HAPPEN?

When a person is won through evangelism, whether by personal contact or in a church service, he then goes through the process of consolidation within 48 hours of his conversion. Everything related to this person is corroborated through a phone call or a visit to his house the following week. Later, he will begin his discipleship where he will be introduced to the ABC's of Christian life. This time is used to prepare the new believer for the Encounter in a stage called, Pre-Encounter.

THE PRE-ENCOUNTER

A series of simple conferences creates an expectation towards what will take place during the 3-day retreat. The need to go through this experience is clarified, doubts that may come to one's mind are removed and any fear or preconceived ideas of this important experience are laid to rest. The Pre-Encounter is spiritually important because it is this stage that the person is made aware of his need to be transformed and totally restored.

THE ENCOUNTER

We gather for three days at a location isolated from the

city because it can be hard to leave behind the people and circumstances from one's routine environment, and from which one often receives negative influences.

Why three days? We believe that it is the right amount of time for the Spirit of God to impact their lives. When Paul had his first encounter with Jesus, he locked his room for three days in Damascus until the prophet Ananias prayed for him so that he could receive his eyesight. When Paul ended his retreat, his heart had been so totally changed that he started to preach about Christ whom he had previously persecuted, leaving even believers confused. In the Encounters, all hindrances preventing the progress of one's Christian life and develop of a fruitful leadership, dies. One certainly dies to his old life, and the anointing for the new guidance in the power of the Holy Spirit is received.

One of the most critical seasons in the life of the patriarch Jacob was when he received news that his brother Esau had sworn to kill him as soon as he saw him, for having stolen his birthright blessing. Historically this blessing was given to the firstborn. Greatly fearing him, Jacob spent many years fleeing from his brother. The news of the encounter he was going to have with his brother horrified him. This made him seek God with all his heart. One night he had a personal encounter with the Lord who revealed Himself in the form of an angel, and he experienced total deliverance in his spirit.

He said, *"For I have seen God face to face, and my life is preserved"* (Genesis 32:30). That encounter changed the panorama of things for Jacob, because when he met his brother, he said, *"...I have seen your face, as though I had seen the face of God..."* (Genesis 33:10). Jacob's encounter with the Lord changed everything.

That was Jacob's true encounter with God. From that point, his life wasn't the same. So must it happen with all who go to an Encounter. Their lives cannot stay the same because in that environment they are totally freed so they can look towards the security of a genuine relationship with the Lord and others.

Chapter Twelve

A VISION FOR WORLD CONQUEST

"The church of the new millennium will be a cellular church with leaders righteously prepared and they will reconcile families with the grace of the Lord." C.C.D.

PREPARING OURSELVES FOR
THE NEW MILLENNIUM

The vision that God has given us is to reach entire nations and conquer the world for Christ. The time has come for Christians to change the course of history of our world with the message of salvation. Today, outstanding leaders from all parts of the world visit our church to study the vision and set it in motion, in their respective nations. In our new millennium, the church will move to conquer people's hearts with leaders righteously prepared to penetrate their homes.

We are in the greatest time of spiritual harvesting, and the following is not a personal pretence, it is a decree given by the Lord to His sons:

"I will declare the decree: the Lord has said to Me, You are My Son, today I have begotten You. Ask of Me, and I will give You nations for your inheritance, and the ends of the earth for Your possession." (Psalm 2:7-8)

Only those of us who have acquired the privilege of being called sons of God for our faith in Jesus Christ can aspire to take possession and conquer entire nations.

THE VISION IS TO UNITE NATIONS

By thoroughly studying the sacred Scriptures, I have discovered a generous God who gives to all abundantly. However, weakness in the heart of man makes everything seem small and limited since man mixes the Word of God with doubt and unbelief. But we still have the opportunity to prove that the Divine vision is not destined for a particular group of people but is available to all nations. That is why we have decided to impact the earth from our nation of Colombia, by taking the best fruit that we have birthed from the revival, that we have been experiencing, and releasing it to the nations.

The Bible teaches us that when God chose the people of Israel it was like a closed circle where salvation was only for Jews. But when Jesus came, that wall of division broke down which enabled unification for the Jews and the Gentiles under God. However, the Jews hardened their hearts and God refused them, whereupon salvation was open to all other nations.

When He was resurrected from the dead, the Lord told His disciples, *"All authority has been given to Me in heaven and on earth. Go therefore and make disciples of all nations..."* Notice, He did not say, "Go therefore and teach in the nations."

"...the kingdom of this world have become the nations of our Lord and of his Christ, and He shall reign forever and ever!" (Revelation 11:15b)

If we believe this is so we must begin the conquest of the nations for Him. The Lord is showing winds of blessing for the world, i.e., political, social and most importantly, spiritual winds of change.

LET'S GET THE CHURCH OUT
OF THE FOUR WALLS

The time has come to stop the confinement of the church between its four walls and among its traditional rites, dogmas and liturgies. God desires a spiritual revolution in His church to change its old mentality, to transmit the live essence of His Spirit so that each believer navigates in the river of His power. Today, the Lord is raising an army of warriors made up of men, women, youth and children who are skilled in using spiritual weapons and in handling the sword of the Word to defeat the adversary and his host of demons in the name of Jesus. Nation conquering requires spiritual warfare:

"Proclaim this among the nations: Prepare for war! Wake up the mighty men, let all the men of war draw near, let them come up, Beat your plowshares into swords and your pruning hooks into spears; let the weak say, 'I am strong.'" (Joel 3:9-10)

The church has been called to be a part of the solution in each country. We are conquerors, victorious people full of faith and men and women of war that in the name of Jesus, say, *"Brothers, when I am weak, the power of God strengthens me."*

The book of Ephesians talks about a church that wars and triumphs but many ignore these realities. Some time ago a missionary visited us, and after traveling throughout our country, they so admired its richness and exclaimed, *"The Colombians are as a beggar who is seated on a chest full of gold while starving. It seems so incredible that Colombia is a country with its own natural resources and the people are starving. There is too much misery and ruin."*

I understand his commentary and I prepared to analyze it spiritually. Many believers are like that beggar and don't take advantage of God's promises. For us and for all nations there is a promise that accompanies the conqueror:

"Blessed be the God and Father of our Lord Jesus Christ, who has blessed us with every spiritual blessing in heavenly places in Christ." (Ephesians 1:3)

By implementing the cellular vision and the principle of the Twelve, we fulfill our part so that the promise of this text becomes a reality in Colombia and in the rest of the world. We also do it by taking our spiritual armor and remembering that at all times we prevail in the name of Jesus under whose feet God subdued principalities, authorities and lordships; including political, economic social and ecclesiastical powers. Christ is the head and as His church we are His entire body and if we open our understanding and renew our minds we must conclude that the devil is under our feet! Another promise is fulfilled when we take the offensive toward conquest, *"And the God of peace will crush Satan under your feet shortly..."* (Romans 16:20a).

AN INSPIRATION FOR ALL NATIONS

The model that God gave us is inspiring entire nations in such a way that all who have adopted it are experiencing unprecedented growth. The anointing of multiplication that the Lord gave us has been transmitted to literally hundreds of leaders around the world and now through this book we also impart it to you. To work in the cellular vision is not difficult because God's anointing is poured out for the task. I have had the wonderful opportunity and privilege of praying for many pastors who have opened their minds and their hearts to allow the vision to find a home in them and their results are a guarantee that we are moving in the proper direction. An American pastor testified to me, *"Since you prayed for me a year ago and transmitted to me the multiplication anointing, my church has grown and its membership has doubled."* I also prayed for a pastor in Costa Rica whose church grew from 500 to 1,5000 members, and from 0 to 300 cells in only nine months. This same vision is being developed in Russia, China, Germany, England, Scotland, Greece, Argentina, Peru, Paraguay, Mexico, Puerto Rico, Canada, United States, Spain, Venezuela, Panama and other countries. Practically the whole world is talking about the model of the Twelve, simply because it represents a strategic way for churches to grow orderly and in significant numbers. The alternative would be a disoriented mass of people who would attend a church service several times and just as they came they would leave. This is without a doubt the model to follow. The testimonies of pastors from around the world testify to its effectiveness in their ministries.

I know that there are many aspects that I have not included in this book, but I am sure that what I have expounded on will be of great help to break old schemes and place your church, its leadership, and your entire ministry in a new dimension of power. The explosion of growth and the conserving of fruit are destined for you and your nation. If you set in motion the principles described in this book your church will enter the new millennium prepared with effective tools to penetrate the hearts of lost souls.

What God has given to our church, the International Charismatic Mission, is a successful formula that I could have reserved exclusively for myself, but the Lord told me clearly, *"Be generous. Don't keep that treasure for yourself.*

Share it with other pastors and with the world." That's why we have opened our doors unselfishly to the nations so that they may receive the vision.

Our desire is for the church of Jesus Christ to grow and mature and that through this vision the impact and transformation of multiplied thousands of lives on every continent of the world will be realized. Years ago I had a vision where God placed in my hands the torch of multiplication and the cellular system. When I received it and started running with it, the church began to multiply. That torch is still lit, *take it and run with it, it is for you too!*